Conversations with Barry Lopez

Conversations with Barry Lopez

Walking the Path of Imagination

By William E. Tydeman

UNIVERSITY OF OKLAHOMA PRESS : NORMAN

Also by William E. Tydeman
(co-editor) *Reading into Photography: Selected Essays, 1959–1980*
  (Albuquerque, 1982)
(co-editor) *Llano Estacado: An Island in the Sky*
  (Lubbock, Texas, 2011)

Library of Congress Cataloging-in-Publication Data
Tydeman, William E., 1942–
Conversations with Barry Lopez: walking the path of imagination
by William E. Tydeman.
    pages   cm
Includes bibliographical references.
ISBN 978-0-8061-4407-8 (pbk.: alk. paper)
1. Lopez, Barry Holstun, 1945– —Interviews. 2. Tydeman, William E., 1942–
—Interviews. 3. Authors, American—20th century—Interviews. 4. Literary form.
5. Memory in literature. I. Title.
PS3562.O67Z88 2013
813'.54—dc23
2013013060

Contents

List of Illustrations   vii

Preface   ix

Introduction   3

The Search for Seamless Coherence
   Finn Rock, Oregon, April 29, 2002   33

Science, the Imagination,
and the Collaborative Search for Form
   Texas Tech University, Lubbock, Texas,
   March 6, 2004   71

Art, Activism, and the Biological Fate
of Communities
   Texas Tech University, Lubbock, Texas,
   March 24, 2007   115

Afterword   147

Works by Barry Lopez,
compiled by Diane Warner   151

Illustrations

Barry Brennan with his mother,
northern California, 1949   61

Barry Lopez and his grandson, Pearl Harbor, April 2012   61

Mary, Barry, and Dennis Brennan, 1951   62

Barry Lopez, graduation portrait,
Loyola High School, 1962   62

Barry and his brother Dennis, Sacré Coeur, Paris,
August 1962   63

Barry at the Cliffs of Moher, Ireland, August 1962   63

Carrying a wolf, Susitna River drainage,
Nelchina Basin, Alaska, March 1976   64

Anaktuvuk Pass, Brooks Range, Alaska, June 1979   64

Anasazi storage room, North Rim
of the Grand Canyon, February 1983   65

Wounded hippo on upper Boro River,
northern Botswana, May 1987   65

Practicing rescue operations, Ross Island,
Antarctica, 1988   66

Barry Lopez with Al Gore, Newall Glacier, Antarctica,
November 1988   67

On Polar Plateau, twenty kilometers from the South Pole,
November 1988   67

Barry Lopez and Tony Beasley, scuba diving,
    Galápagos Islands, March 1991   68

Edward Abbey memorial, Moab, Utah, May 1989   68

Barry Lopez and Alan Magee, Thomaston,
    Maine, October 2002   69

Barry Lopez and David Darling,
    Erie, Colorado, April 1981   69

Barry Lopez and Jim Harrison,
    Wilson, Wyoming, May 1991   70

Barry Lopez and his wife, Debra Gwartney,
    with their grandchildren, Oregon, 2011   70

Preface

I REMEMBER MY FIRST ENCOUNTER with Barry Lopez's work. In Albuquerque, on Cornell Avenue next to the University of New Mexico, behind the still-thriving Frontier Restaurant, sat The Living Batch Bookstore. The Batch was in many ways the hub of literary life in New Mexico in the seventies and eighties. There, on the shelf displaying new books in 1988, I saw a copy of *Crossing Open Ground*. I picked it up, read the dust jacket, and thumbed through a few pages. My eyes settled on a quotation from Maximilian of Wied: "We saw white wolves on the opposite shore and the cranes flew heavily before us." That image stays with me still. I tucked the book under my arm. As I approached the checkout, Gus Blaisdell, the polymath owner of The Living Batch, asked me if I knew Lopez's work. "No," I confessed uneasily. (Gus, with his wide-ranging interests and sharp mind, was a tough fellow to please.) "You'll love it," he said. He was right. Reading the essays, I asked myself time and time again, "How could I have missed his earlier work?"

The radiance of discovery stayed with me. A passage from Lopez's essay "Searching for Ancestors," in *Crossing Open Ground*, appears in my commonplace book with the date April 4, 1989: "One of the great dreams of man must be to find some place between the extremes of nature and civilization where it is possible to live without regret." This is the first in a long string of quotations from his works that I find among my entries there for the eighties and nineties. Many of these words speak to my regret, my failure to find a permanent home. Yet, as I became a student of Lopez's work, I also discovered what the

Buddhists call the three noble principles: "good in the beginning, good in the middle, good at the end." From beginning to end, from cover to cover, the sustained excellence of Lopez's work—the richness, the complexity, the sheer beauty of his quest to examine the mystery of human existence—never fails to delight and educate.

As I worked to help coordinate his work as Visiting Distinguished Scholar at Texas Tech (2003–), I also came increasingly to appreciate Lopez's concerns—what he calls the social obligations of the artist. Robert Coles's account of his first meeting with Dorothy Day could just as easily have been written about Lopez's personal style of interaction. Coles tells of finding Day sitting at a table with a drunken woman. The exchange for him was exasperating.

> I found myself increasingly confused by what seemed to be an interminable, essentially absurd exchange taking place between two middle-aged women. When would it end? The alcoholic ranting and the silent nodding, occasionally interrupted by a brief question, which only served, maddeningly, to wind up the over-talkative one rather than wind her down. Finally silence fell upon the room. Dorothy Day asked the woman if she would mind an interruption. She got up and came over to me: She said, "Are you waiting to talk to one of us?" *One of us*: with those words she had cut through layers of self-importance, a lifetime of bourgeois privilege . . . with those words, so quietly and politely spoken, she had indirectly told me what the Catholic Worker Movement was all about and what she herself was like.

The uniform politeness, the determination to avoid creating enemies, the ability to listen, are hallmarks of Lopez's relationships and encounters with the public.

I also witnessed the evolution of his thinking regarding larger global issues. He once expressed to me his concern about becoming narrowly focused in his work. The nature–culture distinction of the seventies and eighties no longer engaged him: "If you can't see the connection between environmental justice and social justice, you're missing something crucial." I began to realize that his public readings, presentations, and classroom discussions, while intimately connected to his written work, provided a parallel structure to connect with and illuminate his social concerns as a writer. In retrospect, I lament that so many of his talks, readings, and classroom interactions were not recorded. Had I been smarter, we would now have a video archive to parallel his manuscript collection at Texas Tech University.

We began the interviews in 2002. Barry and I shared the view that many facets of his work were unexplored or misunderstood. We made a concerted effort to avoid repeating what had appeared in other published interviews. The interviews that make up this book were tape-recorded, transcribed, and later edited for clarity by Lopez and myself. No other interviews were done. Only as we neared the end of our interviews did I realize that, much like the writer's own work, my luck was to bear witness. Over more than a decade, I was privileged to hear many more of Lopez's talks, public presentations, conversations, and class discussions. Not long into his work at Texas Tech, I began to perceive firsthand his broad faith in the human spirit. I marveled at his ability to bring an audience to life, and I came to understand his belief in the importance of story in stimulating thinking on crucial issues of our time. In this preface I extend an invitation to the reader to follow these themes and to walk the footpath of Lopez's imagination.

I do not see my role in this volume as anything more than that of a compiler. I have not sought to review or critique Lopez's work, so this is not a work of criticism. My hope is that the introduction and the interviews included in this volume will stretch our understanding and help us to discover the pattern of Lopez's work. Flummoxed by how to address concisely the range and sophistication of his thinking, I have sought to relate in the introduction's sequence of anecdotes some incidents and examples that stand for the larger configuration. I think of the structural properties of that assembly of recollections as long-form synecdoche: not a word or a phrase, but a paragraph or a page or two standing for the whole, illuminating the big picture of a writer's work.

Looking back, I now understand the interviews I conducted as one part of my effort to provide a larger stage for the examination of the literature of place and Lopez's quest for reconciliation and social justice. This effort now extends back over a decade. Barry's literary archive was the first to be acquired, in 1999, as part of Texas Tech University's James Sowell Family Collection in Literature, Community, and the Natural World. As other authors' papers have been added to the collection, we've come to see mutual respect, the friendship and feeling of community identity that these writers have shared. The pettiness, "the scrimmage of appetites," as Delmore Schwartz once described it, is entirely absent. Here, literature serves not just a community of writers, readers, and scholars but a community of all living things.

One incident might serve to illustrate this larger configuration of interrelatedness and community. In 2007, on our way north on Interstate 27 to Tule Canyon, artist Richard Rowland, Lopez, and I passed a coyote, dead on the side of the highway. I was intent on getting to the canyon, worrying over our arrangements there. My glance at the coyote was fleeting at best. Barry looked, stiffened, and rose up in his seat. Maybe ten seconds passed. "We've got to go back," he said softly. I turned around. Another exit loomed ahead, and taking advantage of a long stretch of access road, we returned to the dead coyote. I sat stock-still at the wheel, unsure of what to say or do. Barry and Richard jumped out of the car. Without words, Barry nodded his intention to Richard. Richard softly lifted the front paws, Barry the back legs. Slowly, silently, they walked off about twenty-five yards from the roadside. They laid him carefully on the short grass. "Better," Richard said. "He can rest more comfortably there."

The interviews that comprise the main body of this volume were conducted in 2002, 2004, and 2007. Earlier versions of the first and second interviews appeared in *Iron Horse* and *Northwest Review*, respectively.

The material supplied in the introduction is taken from my notes and from various documents, including Lopez's correspondence. The intent of the introduction is to provide a window through which to view Lopez's conversations, lectures, and personal correspondence that were created mostly during his work at Texas Tech University as Visiting Distinguished Scholar. Like the interviews themselves, these anecdotes are arranged in roughly chronological order. Together they demonstrate, I hope, the remarkable continuity and congruence of Lopez's thinking during a writing career that now spans more than forty years.

The biographical sketch that opens the introduction summarizes some of the influences on his writing career but is not meant to stand for a more conventional biography. To satisfy the formal strictures of a biographical treatment would require a book in itself, with expanded structures and layers of emotional depth. The biographical sketch and introductory anecdotes, together with Diane Warner's comprehensive bibliography, will have succeeded if interested readers are drawn toward walking the path of Lopez's imagination in the interviews.

Conversations with Barry Lopez

Introduction

IN THE SPRING OF 1942 John (Jack) Edward Brennan (1905–84), an advertising executive and first-generation Irish Catholic living in the Bronx, New York, abandoned his wife and four-year-old son to marry Mary Frances Holstun (1913–76), in Atlanta, Georgia. Mary, a divorcee who wrote a women's column for the *Birmingham* (Alabama) *News* under the name of Ada Homes, had met Jack in Chicago in November 1940, at a convention of the Outdoor Advertising Association of America. The couple established a residence at The Orienta, an apartment building with a private yacht basin in Mamaroneck, New York, on Long Island Sound. Jack commuted the twenty-five miles by train from there to his offices on Lexington Avenue in Manhattan every day. Their first child, Barry Holstun Brennan, was born on January 6, 1945, in the hospital at Port Chester, New York.

In the fall of 1948, shortly after the birth of a second child, Dennis Patrick Brennan (1948–), the family moved to Reseda, California, a town in the San Fernando Valley in suburban Los Angeles. In 1950 Barry entered the first grade at Our Lady of Grace, a Catholic grammar school in nearby Encino, and in 1951 he and his brother were baptized into the Catholic Church. Jack, who had not divorced his first wife, divorced Mary in 1951 and moved to Miami, Florida, where he was rejoined by his first wife and their thirteen-year-old son John (1938–). Mary bought a small house on Calvert Street in Reseda and began teaching home economics in junior high schools in the San Fernando Valley and at Pierce Junior College in Woodland Hills. She also worked at home as a dressmaker for a small group of private clients.

Mary Brennan took her sons on vacation trips to the eastern and western Mojave Desert, to Tijuana, and regularly to Zuma, Pismo, and other Southern California beaches. The boys spent a season at a summer camp on Big Bear Lake in the California Sierra and part of another with a young park ranger and his wife at the Grand Canyon. Jack did not visit Mary's sons or contact them after his divorce. Years later, he left instructions in his will that they were not to receive any part of his estate.

In December 1955 Mary married Adrian Bernard Lopez (1906–2004), in Las Vegas, Nevada. Adrian, a naturalized American citizen born in Southampton, England, was a twice-divorced New York magazine publisher who vacationed regularly in Southern California. Because her sons were technically the illegitimate children of a bigamous marriage, Mary insisted that Adrian legally adopt the boys after they married. He did, and in 1956 their names were changed to Barry Holstun Lopez and Dennis Holstun Lopez. In June 1956 the boys and their mother moved from Reseda to Adrian's penthouse apartment in a brownstone building he owned in the Murray Hill section of Manhattan. Barry's parents enrolled him in the seventh grade at Loyola School, a private Jesuit prep school for boys on East Eighty-Third Street. He soon became a junior member of the New York Athletic Club and began serving Mass at Our Savior Catholic Church, on Thirty-Eighth Street and Park Avenue. That first August in New York the boys attended St. Regis, a summer camp near Sag Harbor on Long Island's South Fork, where Barry roomed with the writer John Steinbeck's younger son, John. The family began renting a series of summer vacation homes, first at Montauk Point, at the tip of the South Fork, later at Greenwood Lake, New York, and finally at several places on the New Jersey shore. In 1963 Adrian and Mary bought a second home, a beachfront house in Bay Head, New Jersey, near the head of the Intracoastal Waterway.

Mary Holstun Lopez had grown up in a conservative Baptist family in rural Alabama, a culture she began consciously to separate herself from when she married her first husband, an aeronautical engineer, artist, and WPA muralist named Sidney Van Scheck (1899–1978). Van Scheck, a Czech national, had flown a fighter plane for the French during the First World War and in 1935 had designed, for the auditorium at Woodlawn High School in Birmingham, Alabama, the largest WPA mural painted in the American South. After their divorce, Van Scheck moved to California and remarried. When Mary and Jack divorced, Van Scheck and his wife, Grace, befriended Mary, and he and Barry developed a strong relationship. Mary's father, Pleasant Reese Holstun, a gentleman farmer, died before Barry was born, and Barry met Mary's mother, Elizabeth Robinson Holstun, only a few times before she died in September 1966. That he recalls, Barry never met either of Jack's parents. Adrian's father died in 1928, and Adrian's mother, who disapproved of Adrian's third marriage, died several years after he married Mary. In effect, Barry grew up without grandparents.

Following his graduation from Loyola School in June 1962, Barry and his brother traveled across Europe by bus for eight weeks with a small group of students from Loyola. In September Barry enrolled at the University of Notre Dame in South Bend, Indiana, declaring a major in aeronautical engineering. At the end of his first semester at the university he switched his major to communication arts, a change of curriculum that required that he make up coursework in history and English in summer school, which he did at New York University in 1963.

During his sophomore year Barry and his roommate made brief trips regularly by car (against school regulations) to West Virginia, to northern Minnesota, as far south as Mississippi, and west to Missouri. In his early years at Notre Dame, Barry began scripting programs for a show called *Precipice* that he hosted on the college radio station, WSND, and writing short stories. Later he began work in photography and as an actor and technician in the theater program. In the summer of 1964 Barry and his brother embarked on a six-thousand-mile journey across the United States, from Bay Head to the southern California coast, then northward through the western Canadian provinces. They stopped to visit former friends and their old home in Reseda, then worked for a while at a ranch near Moose, Wyoming, operated by the parents of one of Barry's acquaintances. The following June, Barry returned to the ranch in Wyoming, working there as a horse wrangler until he returned to Notre Dame in the fall of 1965 for his senior year.

Barry's first published work began appearing in magazines in the spring of 1966, his senior year at Notre Dame. (See Diane Warner's headnote in the bibliography for additional detail on his early work.) After graduating cum laude from the university in June, Barry traveled to Spain and England with his parents and then, in August, drove to Helena, Montana, where he worked in summer stock theater.

In August 1966, after summer stock theater, Barry returned to New York City and took a job as a college traveler with New American Library, representing their Signet and Mentor lines of paperbacks to college and university professors in the Northeast. While he was on the road in Kentucky for his job in November 1966 he visited Gethsemani, the Trappist monastery near New Hope where Thomas Merton resided, to explore the possibility of a life in that monastic community. He decided against it and drove on to St. Louis, Missouri, where he proposed to Sandra Jean Landers (1946–), a theater major at Webster College whom he had met during her sophomore year at Saint Mary's College in South Bend (where he had also taken theater classes during his senior year at Notre Dame). Barry and Sandra were married on June 10, 1967, at Medford Lakes, New Jersey, near where she lived.

Barry quit his job with New American Library shortly after returning from St. Louis. He went to work as a magazine editor for his stepfather in December 1966, in a two-story building Adrian owned on West Twenty-Sixth Street in Manhattan, its interior little changed from the time when it had been John Jacob Astor III's private bank building. Tension with his stepfather led to Barry's resignation from the firm. That and Sandra's desire to finish her theater degree at Saint Mary's College catalyzed the couple's decision to return to South Bend after the wedding. Barry had been promised employment there as an editor at *Ave Maria* magazine on the Notre Dame campus, for which he had written previously, and as an announcer at WNDU, a commercial radio station also located on the university campus. The couple rented a small house in Mishawaka, Indiana, but when both job offers fell through, Barry signed on for shift work at a local steel mill. He was writing and photographing at this time and was also involved in theater productions at Saint Mary's. In late June 1967 he was unexpectedly offered a full fellowship with a living stipend from the Graduate Department of Education at Notre Dame. He accepted, took his name off the hire list at the steel mill, and began work toward a master of arts in teaching, with an emphasis in English.

In the spring of 1968 Barry and John Tuohey, a journalist and illustrator Barry knew from his undergraduate days, co-founded *Focus Michiana* in South Bend, one of the first city magazines in the country. In August 1968, after editing the first three issues with John, Barry resigned and with Sandra moved to Eugene, Oregon, to begin work on a master of fine arts degree in creative writing at the University of Oregon. After a single term in the MFA program, he switched to a master's degree program in the university's School of Journalism for two terms before withdrawing from the university to write and photograph full-time. In June 1970 Sandra finished a master's degree in library science at the University of Oregon, and the couple moved into a house on the upper McKenzie River, forty miles east of Eugene, where Barry still lives. Barry and Sandra separated in 1996 and divorced in 1999.

While a student at the University of Oregon, Barry collected and rewrote a series of Native American trickster stories, working under the direction of an influential mentor, Barre Toelken, a professor who taught American folklore and Native American studies in the English department. Toelken would later write an introduction for this manuscript, Barry's first book, *Giving Birth to Thunder, Sleeping with His Daughter* (1978). In the early seventies Barry completed the collection of fictional pieces that comprise his second (but first to be published) book, *Desert Notes*, which Sheed, Andrews & McMeel, a Kansas City publishing house, brought out in 1976. The publisher there, Jim Andrews, had been one of Barry's early editors at *Ave Maria* magazine, in 1966.

Jim Andrews published *Giving Birth to Thunder* and subsequently *River Notes* (1979), but he urged Barry, in 1976, to find a New York publisher for his first major book, *Of Wolves and Men* (1978). Barry presented the text and layouts for this book to Scribner and was soon working with Laurie Graham, his longtime editor there. In addition to *Of Wolves and Men*, they would work together on *Winter Count* (1981), *Arctic Dreams* (1986), and *Crossing Open Ground* (1988).

In the mid-seventies Peter Schults, the founder of Photo Researchers, an agency in New York that represented Barry's photographic work, began representing his literary work as well. Barry stopped photographing in September 1981, for reasons he cited in a 1998 essay, "Learning to See." The agency continued to represent his early work and from it earned income for him for decades afterward. In 1985 Schults suggested that Barry seek out a more experienced literary agent, and Barry established a personal and professional relationship with Peter Matson, a co-founder of Sterling Lord Literistic, who has represented him since that time.

Barry made his first trip to the Far East in 1985, visiting Japan and the Philippines. By then he had traveled extensively through Arctic North America and western Europe and had visited every U.S. state but Hawai'i. He subsequently traveled farther afield in eastern Asia, to central Asia, the Middle East, and the Balkans, throughout Australia, through southern and East Africa, the Caribbean and South America, and widely across Antarctica and the Pacific. He also returned to Europe several times.

At the time of Jack Brennan's death in 1984, Barry's half-brother, John Brennan, learned for the first time that he had two half-siblings. He did not know their gender, their ages, or their names, but through a remarkable act of intuition he located Barry in 1998. He and Dennis and Barry have been in regular, close contact ever since.

In 1989 Barry left Scribner and went to work with Elizabeth Sifton at Knopf. When she resigned, Barry continued there with Bobbie Bristol, with whom he published *Field Notes* (1994). When she retired from Knopf, he began work with his current editor, Robin Desser. Together they have produced *About This Life* (1998), *Light Action in the Caribbean* (2000), and *Resistance* (2004). In 1988 Barry had approached North Point Press in San Francisco about publishing *Crow and Weasel* (1990), a novella-length fable illustrated by Tom Pohrt. His editor there, Barbara Ras, later moved on to the University of Georgia Press, where she published a hardback edition of one of Barry's short stories, "Lessons from the Wolverine," illustrated by Tom Pohrt (1997) and a hardback edition of one of his essays, "Apologia," illustrated by Robin Eschner (1998).

During the seventies, eighties, and nineties Barry received a number of awards and honors, including the National Book Award (1987) for *Arctic Dreams*, the John Burroughs Medal for *Of Wolves and Men* (1978), the first St. Francis of Assisi Award from DePaul University (2002), fellowships from the Guggenheim Foundation (1987), the Lannan Foundation (1990), and the National Science Foundation (1987, 1988, 1991, 1992, 1999), the Orion Society's John Hay Medal (2002), and awards from the American Academy of Arts & Letters (1987), the Academy of Television Arts and Sciences (2004), and the MacDowell Colony (2004). In 2002 he was elected a Fellow of the Explorers Club, and in 2010 he was named the Association of American Geographers' Honorary Geographer for 2011.

In 2002 Barry began editing, with Debra Gwartney (1957–), *Home Ground* (2006), a literary guide to landscape terms comprising original work from forty-five American poets and writers, which was published by Barbara Ras, who had been newly appointed the director of Trinity University Press in San Antonio, Texas. On December 15, 2007, Debra and Barry were married in Santa Fe, New Mexico, in a small ceremony attended by Debra's four daughters and two grandchildren, by Barry's brothers, and by some of the couple's circle of friends in New Mexico.

In the spring of 2010 Barry temporarily stopped writing short fiction and essays for magazines in order to concentrate on a short memoir about his childhood, called "Sliver of Sky," and a long nonfiction manuscript, provisionally entitled *Horizon: The Autobiography of a Journey*.

I
Undated

Early in his twice-yearly visits to Texas Tech, Lopez asked to visit the National Ranching Heritage Center (NRHC), a museum and historical park of thirty acres on the north boundary of the Texas Tech campus. It contains thirty-eight full-size structures representing the evolution of Texas ranch life. Each building—dugouts, corrals, a train depot—is representative of the original geographical location from which it was moved.

We arrived, signed the guest book and greeted the uniformed guard. As we made our way along the pathway to the featured buildings, I chattered away about ranching history and NHRC's creation. Lopez endured about fifteen minutes of my chit-chat. Then I realized he hadn't said a word. When I glanced over at him, I was taken aback by the intensity of his gaze—locked in, fully absorbed, eyes moving over every detail. The power of this gaze created what seemed like a ring of energy. I instantly felt he was seeing things that I didn't. Scary. Clearly, my nervous monologue was annoying. Lopez continued to say nothing. I kept quiet.

Later that evening, we talked about the tour. Lopez had a number of observations and questions. By then, I was remembering his work with indigenous people—his mastery of powerful ways to see. He had mentioned in several earlier conversations with me the silence and intense focus that characterize indigenous ways of seeing. The time for talk was at night, perhaps around a campfire, not while traveling through the country.

I witnessed that same intensity whenever we explored Native American sacred landscapes. On a trip to the Adobe Walls battle site in 2010, I overheard him talking to a student about the place's "sonic landscape"—the wind in the grass, the crackle of fallen leaves underfoot, the swish of pants over the brush. "These can be anchors in your story," he said to her. "They can provide a structure."

As I listened to Lopez's advice I had a thought. The immersion in detail and the role played by sound, wind, and space, when combined with what light brings to the eye, are all elements of the power to see more. Brought deftly together within the temporal arc of the long view and placed within the space of the big picture, this structured integration helps readers discover a way through experience. Part of Lopez's creativity, I thought, comes from what photographers call observational focal length. Up close, the focus is on unseen detail, but detail that, combined within a broad overview of other details, integrates the sweep of the scene, moving it toward panorama and the *longue durée*. Few writers can do both.

II
Undated

Lopez's words from my notebooks:

"I edit my work myself. I write and then edit three or four times. When I hand it over to someone else I hope for it to be flawless."

"I can feel the story in my hands. When I am at the typewriter I see my hands come to rest. We're done. This is as good as I can make it."

"Good language has to find a good subject."

"I was two years into the research for *Arctic Dreams* before I wrote an outline. I knew, finally, what I was going to continue to work on and what I was going to let go!"

"I see images—artistic imagery, historical imagery—extended in an arc."

"I worked on the first draft [for *Arctic Dreams*] section by section, in order, twelve sections, each section taking about four weeks. The first draft of the book took me a year, three to four months for the second draft, two months on the third, one month on the fourth. Then eight days for the final draft."

The day he finished the final draft, Lopez said to a friend, "Is the fifth draft of *Arctic Dreams* any good? I have no idea, but whatever it is, I respect it. Is it beautiful? I don't know, but it's a good piece of work, no matter what the commercial world eventually says."

"Do I help make the world safe and beautiful by what I do?"

III
March 10, 2004

As a part of the Presidential Lecture Series at Rice University in 2004, Lopez spoke on the topic of learning to see. The address was "Learning to See: Artistic Collaboration and the Human Community." Walter Isle, in a fine introduction of the speaker, spoke of the central theme in Lopez's work: strengthening the nature/culture connection. As the presentation progressed, Lopez suggested that the central theme among artists and writers of place was a search for community. I'd often marveled at his willingness to give full attention and a warm hand of support to many businessmen, politicians, and ordinary folk who don't share his political, ethical, or moral views. As he enumerated the threats to community in what he labeled "a singular time of concern," he was careful to say: "I don't believe the situation is anyone's fault." When he suggested that "here's a thought about finding and destroying the enemy," I listened with full attention. "I don't believe there is an enemy," he said. "This is what history teaches: if you spend your energy trying to identify an enemy, and you track down this putative enemy, and you kill him, he will rise again in another quarter, in another costume. And should you be seduced a second time, you'll be at it again. By then you'll be completely worn out. And what you swore your life to—to establish something beautiful once you've destroyed the enemy, you will not have the energy to begin. The thing to do is to make the enemy irrelevant."

In the same lecture he also talked about individual genius. I'd heard him speak about individual genius often. I confess that I was never convinced that he himself owed everything in his work to influences in the community. Perhaps because I thought too often about some of community's polar opposites—individual talents, individual technical skills—I was especially keen to hear more. He opened with, "I have been puzzled and troubled all my life by the idea of individual genius." I'd never heard him cast the issue in this large a context. A lifelong problem? He pushed his glasses back on his nose, brushed his hand across his mouth, and went on: "In my experience those who are most comfortable with this characterization are often the people who are least aware of how their work has benefited from the support of others. In my view they are always ready to accept full credit for the quality of an individual vision but are vaguely contemptuous of the idea that something they've made is not fully their own, that it is partly due to the way people support them and also to something unknown moving through them. We say Bach is a genius. But when Yo-Yo Ma finds two different interpretations of the *Sixth Cello Suite*, what is Ma? I don't mean to be academic here or to play games with concepts of originality or interpretation. I'm saying something much simpler, or, you might say, more naive. It is my view that individual genius is a gift, that the gifted personality is the manifestation of a kind of genius that belongs, finally, to the community. The genius is in *us*."

"In ensemble art," he continued, "the theater, dance, the music of the quartet, the trio, the orchestra, it is easy to see that one person is not responsible. It's harder with painting, photography, or writing. Why pursue this distinction? Because in a celebrity-driven culture like ours, claims to originality and genius seem curiously misplaced. Historically, humanity has more often benefited from the genius of the community than from the genius of the individual. And people with no faith in their own wisdom in hard times have perished waiting for a genius to appear and lead them."

He added, "I believe in the singular vision of the individual artist. If I am honest, I would have to say I accept the artist's occasional disregard for community, the neglect of spouse, of children and parents, that this obsession sometimes entails. But there is a line here. What does the community gain by your work, and what does it lose? The line I draw for myself here is, I know, subjective and probably inconsistent. What is more on my mind these days about this though . . . is this. If humanity is imperiled, shouldn't our investment in the work of artists include more than it does? Shouldn't we be underwriting collaboration and cooperation? If, as the poet Robert Duncan has said, 'The drama of our time is the coming of all men into one fate,' shouldn't we be thinking more about a wisdom revealed in the mounting of one communal voice . . . ?

"In some strange way, I think we are at a cultural crossroads today where the primacy of the individual is concerned. If we are endangered as a culture, do we need to ask ourselves what price society pays for our vigorous support of individual visions? I don't know. I do not really worry about what other people are doing. In my own life, however, I am suspicious of this idea, the primacy of the individual, despite my Enlightenment upbringing. So, I am trying to explore the disquieting dimensions of my own ego."

IV

May 13, 2005

The Honors College at Texas Tech holds an annual graduation dinner. It's a gala occasion. Graduates radiate excitement; proud parents beam with pleasure. After the usual welcoming remarks, the meal is served buffet style. Around the clatter of plates and utensils comes a steady buzz of animated conversation. Once the din has subsided (the festivities take place in a large banquet room in the Lubbock Civic Center), Lopez is introduced by the Dean of the Honors College, Gary Bell. Lopez is dressed in his usual "business" attire—artfully, it seems to me. Cowboy boots, slacks, a blue blazer, grey button-down shirt, and light purple tie. His silver wrist band, heavily laced in turquoise, and a black belt with silver ornamentation complete his attire. I think how perfectly at ease he seems in these clothes.

He steps to the podium and eyes turn his way. He asks the indulgence of all present to speak directly to the students. In the expectant quiet, he speaks with a careful flourish, emphasizing certain sentence endings, changing his modulation, introducing pauses. His remarks are eloquent and carefully chosen. His message deals with what it means to be knowledgeable and truly educated. What does it mean to find meaningful and dignified work? He offers the traits of responsibility, reciprocity, and reverence. "With these three things in place, communities thrive," he says. "Without them, civilizations collapse." He warns the students about overestimating the value of a college education. "Don't be led into the belief that a man or women with no degree isn't worth the same undivided attention you've come to give those whom you regard as your very well-educated colleagues and peers. The issue in life is to make common cause with knowledgeable people, which, if my own experience is sufficient enough testimony for you, means common cause with a fair number of people who never entered college."

He concludes with, "What I am saying, I think, is obvious. Do not fall into the trap of overvaluing your degree—or your social standing because of that degree—so that you distain the counsel of those who have no degrees. Look always for the *knowledgeable* person—and hold yourself to that standard."

The graduating students nod their heads and smile. Whispers grow as parents and students share their pleasure at these remarks. I think back to all the honors classes Lopez has addressed since 2003. The speech seems an apt send-off. Students have told me over the years that his voice and wisdom will always be with them.

V
October 31, 2005

As Distinguished Visiting Scholar, Lopez regularly meets with classes and professors. Often, I attend, knowing his remarks will be provocative. On this Halloween, Lopez is speaking with a creative writing class taught by Jackie Koslov-Wenthe. The flow of ideas and the range of material presented leaves me dazzled. I wonder how he always manages to find a structure that makes profound ideas more comprehensible.

In his presentation Lopez states two things that bring me up short. Predictably, he fields questions on the differences between his literary nonfiction and fiction. "Revision in nonfiction for me is about making the original expression of the idea more thoughtful," he says. In fiction, "first drafts are not really about thinking. Fiction for me is much less intentional."

He goes on to connect memory and literary form, mentioning Eduardo Galeano's obsession with memory. "The writer is the servant of memory," Galeano reminds us. And misrepresentation of the self in nonfiction should be considered irresponsible, even unethical, if the writer deliberately makes up material. As the students' questions continue, Lopez suggests, almost as an aside, that he has learned nothing in his life that caused him to doubt his relationship with the Divine.

Later he posits a connection between what we know and the larger societal issues we face. He continues, "Use the material, the images and ideas that developed during your youth. Don't be afraid to use what you know to address the big issues, like the political power of the state and the absence of justice."

As he speaks, I close my eyes and see a set of scrapbooks. The shape and color are indistinct. They open to artfully cropped and mounted tear sheets of polar bear photos. I'm reminded that Lopez once told me that the scrapbooks he made in his youth reflected what would become the concerns and interests of his adult years. I've never seen the scrapbooks, but I'm intrigued by this continuity and congruence that seem to have lasted a lifetime. Later, it also occurs to me that the last of the interviews presented in this volume concludes with a discussion of scrapbooks, a strong signal perhaps, of the need for further investigations.

When I begin listening again, Lopez is speaking about our culture's lack of dependable narrative structures, returning to one of his central themes: storytelling. He emphasizes that in traditional storytelling there is often no spatiotemporal separation. A distinction between them is not made. There is a unity in time and space. "Storytelling is a form of pattern-making," he says. "Like music or dance or painting." Storytelling addresses dissonance in a community. The storyteller illuminates these difficulties without indicting anyone. "Indictment is pointless. The writer searches, rather, for the relationships that will take care of us." Our common predicaments are part of the story of being human.

The students listen well. Heads nod. Pens move across the page. Lopez concludes by saying, "For the storyteller to engage in storytelling is an ethical obligation."

VI
2007

As part of a larger video project entitled *Barry Lopez: Working Writer*, Lopez sits down with filmmaker Judy Oskam. He has just finished a reading. The conversation drifts toward the challenges of creating form and structure. As I listen, I remember that Lopez said it took two years of work to discover the structure for *Arctic Dreams*. He speaks to the camera without a hesitation or pause. The words come easily, almost ready for the page. He tells Oskam, "You can't understand anything without structure. I gravitate toward structure. But I have to *discover* structure. . . . The hardest thing in nonfiction is to discover a structure that will hold the material in an almost weightless way, so that the reader is able to move through a story replete with information but does not feel burdened. Why? Because the structure suspends everything weightlessly."

VII
February 23, 2006

Lopez spoke at a conference sponsored by Texas Tech's Southwest Center. In a half-hour address, he identified his theme in the form of a question. "Why are we so little interested in what others outside our race, outside our religion, outside our culture, outside our gender, outside our time, even outside our field have to say? . . . Why are we so little interested in the literary imaginations of the peoples indigenous to North America?"

He went on to offer one of his fullest explanations of his concept of a literary imagination: "I should say what I mean by a literary imagination. I am inclined to say that it is the ability to think in tropes, but this is finally redundant. So I will say that to have a literary imagination is to think about all that was and is happening around you as a story, or stories. You imagine these events and the emotions that they provoke collapsing into tropes, something as obscure as synecdoche, and you think of all the musical potential in poetry—meter, rhyme, alliteration, assonance—but especially you think of metaphor. Event and emotion collapse into a language enhanced by tropes. The effort here is to tell a story, and thereby achieve illumination, meaning, a healed spirit, and the revitalization of our memories.

"If you will let me leave it at that—a literary imagination thinks of the world as knowledge through story—I'd be grateful."

Later in that same address, he returned to this theme, making an appeal for incorporating indigenous philosophy into our political discussion. "When Emerson remarked that Thoreau wanted to be an Indian, he was alluding to Thoreau's suspicion that without a guiding indigenous philosophy—an ethic, an epistemology, an aesthetic, a logic and a metaphysics—grounded in a specific place, no system of governance or economics would survive the threats implicit in new innovations. Whether you find yourself in agreement with this insight or not," Lopez said, "it would seem the very essence of wisdom, given the nature of the present we are living in, to inquire among the traditional people of North America, to ask them what they make of where we are, to invite their voices to be heard at the highest levels of decision making."

VIII
March 3, 2007

In 2004 Lopez wrote a book review of *Shem Pete's Alaska*. It was his first book review in twelve years. We were on our way out of town together, heading for New Mexico. Lopez was driving. I asked him why he wrote so few reviews. "I'm not a good critic," he said. "I'm too harsh on what I don't respect and too quick to praise what I admire. I don't have the necessary balance." His usual practice, early on, was to write in longhand and then go to the typewriter for later drafts and corrections. "Except for book reviews," he said, "which I always began at the typewriter. That told me I wasn't giving it the right kind of depth . . . so I just quit doing it."

IX
March 3, 2007

We continued our trip to Santa Fe with stops at a wildlife refuge in Fort Sumner and an inspection of the Blue Hole, a center for scuba divers in Santa Rosa. Lopez had spent a good part of the previous week at Texas Tech meeting with classes and planning projects. That evening, in Santa Fe, Chip Blake of the Orion Society and Lopez spoke to a group of *Orion* magazine supporters. The Orion Society is one of the key American organizations promoting examination of the relationship between nature, community, and social justice. After Blake outlined possible new directions for the Orion Society, Lopez spoke. It is one of his most personal talks, referring directly to the issue of reverence and love. Environmental activism is "not about a romance with ideals," he says. "It's about reciprocity. If you cannot be in love, you are a burden to society." He suggests we must rekindle the memory of proper conduct that leads to love. He raises a question, "How can I create intimacy?" He further suggests, "The fruit of intimacy is hope. We must find ways to break down the barriers between ourselves and a reawakened sense of the power to do good in the world. With the dark horseman on the horizon, we must carefully seek intimacy, closeness, trust, vulnerability in all that we do. Like the Navajo, we can think and sing our reality into being."

X
December 5, 2008

We are in a meeting with Texas Tech University Press to discuss Lopez's suggestion that the Press develop a publication series around the theme of reconciliation. Robert Mandel, director of the Press, and Judith Keeling, the acquisitions editor, are keenly interested. We sit across from each other, around a long conference table. I stare at bookshelves filled with Texas Tech University Press books published over the years. Lopez suggests that the series should begin with a selection of essays, stories, and poems from two recent issues of *Manoa*, a journal of international writing, that have been devoted to reconciliation. I listen to the conversation, but my eyes drift back to the beauty of those Press books—the symmetry, the spines, the dust jackets awash in color. Lopez is talking about books that alter our thinking, move us farther along on the path of reconciliation. For the seminar we held with faculty during Lopez's visit we had read, at his suggestion, *A Human Being Died That Night*, by Pumla Gobodo-Madikizela, a woman who served on the Truth and Reconciliation Committee in South Africa. He mentions the book to Mandel and Keeling and then says in a louder voice, in a timbre that ties the words together in a string of emotion, "I want to ignite people. Set their hair on fire."

XI
April 18, 2009

If location is everything in business, the local International House of Pancakes couldn't be in a better place. Conveniently situated across the street from Texas Tech near the intersection of two busy thoroughfares, it is the gathering place for at least one morning's breakfast during Lopez's visits to campus. The group is usually the Honors College faculty who teach in Texas Tech's Natural History/ Humanities (NHH) undergraduate curriculum. Today, Susan Tomlinson, the program coordinator; Gary Bell, Dean of the College; Mark McGinley, a biologist; Kurt Caswell, who teaches literature and creative writing; and I gather to discuss the NHH program. It's a good group, seemingly immune from what Freud termed "the narcissism of small differences." Ever since Lopez and E. O. Wilson, the famed Harvard biologist, wrote a white paper outlining a structure for the NHH program, Lopez has been actively involved in its growth and challenges. However, the breakfast conversation isn't always about the curriculum.

Today the conversation takes an unexpected turn as Lopez talks about beauty. I'd often heard him talk about beauty. We are both great admirers of the Navajo world view and their philosophy of the Beauty Way, but I'd never heard him build a linkage directly to religion. Inspiration for the artist, he suggested, is the celestial coming through the terrestrial. Access to the eternal is by way of deep entry into the present. "To be inspired is to feel God funneling into one's work. We always want light from the darkness. We know something is there," he says, "before we see it." (I recalled him telling me on an earlier occasion that to build anything beautiful he has to go deep into his own guts.) "The objective for a writer is to try to get some part of the face of God on a piece of paper. It is a fearful undertaking." Everyone nods when Lopez describes the process as "going into something profound without knowing what you are looking for. Beauty is incomprehensible. Isn't that what God is?"

Our food arrives. We drink coffee and concentrate on the plate-sized pancakes. The conversation drifts into a discussion of the beautiful versus the attractive. We cover some of the more familiar themes of beauty as coherence and pattern. As we get up to leave, Lopez suggests that what we all want is to restore beauty. "Witnessing the loss of beauty and the enduring effort to restore beauty, isn't this God?"

XII
April 18, 2009

Lopez tells me a story about the headmaster from his preparatory school, the Loyola School in Manhattan, visiting him at his home in rural Oregon. "It must have been thirty years ago. In the course of the visit, we went for a walk in the woods surrounding my house. My old headmaster said, 'Do you know how fortunate you are?' I said, 'Do you mean because I live in this beautiful place?'

'No,' he responded, 'because you did what you wanted to do. You are doing what you love. Your classmates are all very successful. They're doctors, lawyers, and accountants. But they don't love what they are doing.'"

XIII
December 7, 2009

Many of Barry Lopez's collaborations are with musicians. Even though he is often at pains to remind my composer wife that he doesn't read music, his interests in sonic landscapes and in the structural properties of composed music are well known. He told me once, "Music is very important to me as a writer. Controlling connotation in a sentence is hard to do, but you can do it with music." I recall as well a talk to a creative writing class. He told the students, "I remember once, in the Croydon Museum in Nairobi, the anthropologist Alan Walker was showing me a series of Australopithecine skulls, three million years old, and he put one of his hands on one of the tiny craniums and said, 'Barry, I know that we sang before we spoke.' I often think of that moment, when I consider how deeply we are affected by the tone of language someone uses. And how poetry affects us, the sound of the lines. The *sound* of the language, even on paper, is very powerful."

I wanted to explore the musical connection more completely as it relates to the issue of sound. I asked about a literature text I'd heard him mention before, Laurence Perrin's *Sound and Sense*. Lopez explained that he'd used the book as a freshman at Notre Dame in the fall of

1962. He went on, "I was fascinated by the way sound could convey a sense of something. The focus of the book was on poetry, but it spoke to me about prose, too. I still have my copy of it, and I retain a great deal of information from it—consciously and unconsciously. . . . If you asked me to recall anything specific, I would say, yes, things like how you can really end a sentence by using a hard consonant like a 'k' or a 'd'. If you use an open vowel like an 'o', the sentence continues on, even if you see the period at the end of the sentence. So there were things like that in it. And things about altering the length of sentences in a stanza, which I immediately carried over into the prose."

I wanted to pursue the issue a bit more. I read him a sentence from *Arctic Dreams*: "His lips stretched to the steaming hot surface of the tea and in the chill air I heard the susurrations of his sipping." I ask if the sounds of the "s" in the sentence were a conscious decision. He responded, "I don't know that I was working consciously there, in the sense that you might mean 'consciously.' I wanted sound and rhythm. When you began reading this to me, I started hearing the rest of the sentence right away. 'Susurration' and the 'steaming,' that alliteration, is an example of a *conscious* effort to bring sound into the meaning of the sentence. I resist a little bit the idea that it was *unconscious*, but I don't know. I might go back into a sentence when I'm rewriting because my *unconscious* ear is telling me, 'Put in one more "s" on this run.'"

XIV
December 7, 2009

I ask Lopez about his career trajectory, curious about whether his work might have turned in a different direction, toward the visual or performing arts. He answers with his usual clarity and in great depth. "Here are some initial thoughts. When I read a catalog for a retrospective show by a British artist named Richard Long, who was born in the same year I was, I was so struck by his feeling for space and his desire to make lines in space, these great long walks of his, that I thought with just a little bit of tweaking in my personal history, this could have been an artistic endeavor similar to my story.

"What have I done as an artist? I worked in the theater, I acted, I enjoyed that. I did summer stock in Helena, Montana, at the old Brewery Theatre. I remember after *Arctic Dreams* came out, in the wake of all that attention, I said to myself, 'I don't want to talk to anybody about anything anymore, and I don't want to write anything anymore. I want to work in silence on large pieces of sculpture, in settings in the woods around my house.' I've tried a few pieces like this, in the woods, but there is no real presence, no power in them.

"It's obvious that something in me wants constantly to be engaged in spatial relationships of some sort. There is that opening scene in the introduction in *Desert Notes*. It has to do with a van I was driving at the time. . . . Jim Andrews [his editor] said, 'Tell that story in *Desert Notes*.' I said, 'No, *Desert Notes* is a work of fiction, and this really happened.' And he said, 'No, no, no. It has to be in there.' I did as he asked, creating a nonfiction opening to a work of fiction; but what I was doing with that van on a desert playa was similar to what Robert Long was doing, walking across huge vistas, dealing with big open spaces. I was drawn to deserts and the Arctic because they were what I would call 'classic' rather than 'baroque' landscapes. They offered my imagination a stage. I visualize big movements through space all the time when I am driving. When I drive from Oregon to Denver, say, or somewhere like that, I deliberately plot an *indirect* path, to swoop in like a hawk. I go miles out of the way because I want the feeling of making that kind of oblique approach, rather than just driving the straight line.

"One morning in Fairbanks, the only time I ever flew a plane, a friend asked me to come along on a flight to Bettles. Flying back, he said, 'Do you want to fly the plane?' Yes, I said, I'd love to fly the plane. I was sitting in the co-pilot's seat. I took the stick and began swooping through the raw space, making these big long curves, dropping way down on a banking turn, then gaining altitude again. While I was doing this he said, 'Every once in a while I let somebody fly the plane. Almost everyone flies it in a straight line, holding the compass bearing. They don't turn left or right. They keep asking if it's going along okay. You, you just started flying, really flying, swooping down and following the river—which you realized *is* the compass bearing.' So there is something about that kind of involvement with space that excited me when I read about Richard Long's work, walking through these spaces.

"If you go back and look at an early story like 'The Orrery' [in *Winter Count*], you can see this focus I have on the way objects are arranged in space. These things turn up constantly in my work. Look at a chapter like 'The Country of the Mind,' in *Arctic Dreams*, where the narrator, walking on Pingok Island, heads for a place, circles back, then goes to another place and circles back.

"When I began working as a photographer, I was a literalist infatuated with the sublime. I never pushed through to what lay beyond the sublime. And this brings up for me, of course, Ahab's speech in 'The Quarterdeck' [in *Moby-Dick*], when he says he wants to break through a pasteboard mask. That's what I want to do, in my own life and in my own work, to break through some kind of facade into another plane. I was able to make some photographs in which I did that. I broke through the veil of the sublime into something else, the space behind. I never said anything about doing this in 'Learning to See' because it wasn't apparent to me back then. It's just recently that I've thought, 'Your problem as a photographer was that you couldn't break through the conventionally beautiful, the conventionally sublime.' So I never truly became a photographer. I was a person who was making pictures, but I wouldn't call myself a photographer."

I was puzzled. I asked Lopez where such a breakthrough would lead. Where would it take you? "The breakthrough," he replied, "would be into a place where something was emerging from the photograph that, for me, was extremely powerful, something emerging from what appeared to be an innocuous landscape. A photograph of mine I'm thinking about is of a large weeping willow, growing in an abandoned corral in a small town in eastern Oregon—the way the light was hitting it. It is almost always for me a matter of the appraising light rather than the object. I stopped the truck and drove back and got out my camera and photographed and photographed. There was a way in which the sunlight was driving into and through the tree that was alternately pulling it out of the sky behind it and crushing it, pushing it back. . . . But there are only a few photographs like that. Maybe I thought at the time, 'Boy! This is going to be a lot of work.' Maybe I didn't have the courage. Maybe I didn't want to take the risk, because I didn't know what would happen to my writing.

"When I was a kid, six or seven, an itinerant salesman came to our home in Reseda, California. This was a thing people were interested in in California at that time. He asked the head of household—my mother—if there were children in the house and would the children like to learn to play steel guitar, Hawaiian guitar. The guy would listen and then usually say, 'Well . . . your son has a real aptitude for this. Would you like to sign him up for lessons?' But the guy said right away I had no musical aptitude. None. Still, I've wanted to play music for a long time. Maybe one day I'll do it."

XV
December 2009

I brought up the nickname his Inuit friends had given him—*naa-javaarsuk*, the Ivory Gull. I knew something of this gull's behavior. Lopez reminded me that in *Arctic Dreams* he devoted several paragraphs to its remarkable adaptation to arctic ice floes. A few days later when I went back and reread the passage, I was reminded of his admonition to students and writers: "Go deep." I'd spent several hours in my home library reading about the ivory gull. Yet in Lopez's account there were key pieces of information I'd not seen elsewhere about the gull's beak and how its shorter legs help it conserve heat and how it utilizes the sun's warmth. I told him I knew that this gull often seemed to arrive out of nowhere, dropping from great heights. But this didn't seem to explain why his Inuit friends would call him this nickname. He patiently answered. "This small gull stands off to the side at butchering sites of seal guts, observing the bigger gulls fighting and claiming their share of the gut piles. The ivory gull steps in carefully, picks something up and then retreats." He went on: "So their observation about me was, that I was someone who participated in what they were doing, but somehow I was always stepping back to observe what they were doing. The name they gave me illuminates the challenges of writing literary nonfiction: how to manage the participant's direct involvement and the observer's detached point of view."

I asked, "Did your Inuit friends also know that this gull that nests at the top of world is today one of the animals most threatened by global warming?" "They know," Lopez answered. "*Pagophilia*, the ice lover, depends on sea ice. Scientists tell us the melting of sea ice is changing their environment three to five times faster than any other region of the earth. As the ice cover shrinks so does the ivory gull's access to a food base. Fewer gulls return each year to cliff nesting sites in places where the ice is retreating.

"The melting of arctic ice," he went on, "is the greatest long-term threat to ivory gull populations. Scientists studying nesting ivory gull populations in Canada and Norway have also recently found in the gulls' eggs a high concentration of banned chemicals—mercury, DDT, and other industrial pollutants." He concluded, "Difficulty finding food and the uptake of toxic pollutants influence reproductive behavior. So, where is the future?"

Time and time again I recall Lopez's words to the Natural History/Humanity majors at Texas Tech University: "I am not optimistic. But I am hopeful." Called to act by the powerful messages of Lopez and his fellow writers on the natural world, I wondered, can we summon the hope and imaginative acts to create a future for these birds and ourselves? "Our hope," Lopez has said, "is in each other, not in a long and fruitless wait for genius to save us. And our hope does not lie with technology. It lies with imagination."

Most times when Lopez speaks of hope I am reminded of the simple-minded approach so many critics and intellectuals take toward place-based writing and its expression of hope. They wish to pigeonhole writers of place and claim that hope is a one-dimensional approach, even Pollyannaish and unsophisticated. Lopez, and I, agree with an analysis made by Christopher Lasch, who conveys a nuanced view of the multilayered meaning of hope. He argues that "Hope . . . asserts the goodness of life in the face of its limits." Hope does not require a belief in progress or prevent us from expecting the worst but, rather, hope "trusts life without denying its tragic character. Progressive optimism, often confused with hope, is based on a denial of the natural limits of human power and freedom—a blind faith that things will somehow work out for the best. It is not an effective anecdote to despair." Those who challenge the status quo and support the popular uprising for social justice "require hope, a tragic understanding of life, the disposition to see things through." Hope is what we need.

XVI
February 19, 2006
The Sacred Landscape

The plan was to gather clay and animal bones in "the quiet, most respectful way possible." I was apprehensive. On our first visit to Tule Canyon in the spring of 2005, things hadn't gone well. Our local guide hadn't called ahead to the ranch foreman to clear our visit to this historic site where 1,400 horses were captured at Palo Duro Canyon and 1,100 taken south to Tule Canyon and killed by U.S. cavalrymen in 1874. (Comanche and Kiowa were attacked on September 28 of that year in nearby Palo Duro Canyon, and their horses were confiscated for slaughter or redistribution to federal troops.) The foreman came roaring up to us in his ATV loaded for bear. Horses corralled at the edge of the canyon near the house barn shifted nervously and whinnied. Our arrival seemed to disturb the canyon's sacred silence. There were too many people: two videographers, a field historian, a local history expert, Lopez, and myself. The purpose of this visit was to make a reconnaissance, to break the boundary of the unknown. We wanted to determine if Lopez's idea to gather clay and bone here and to use them in a reconciliation ceremony was feasible.

We stayed only long enough for Lopez to determine that the canyon, ground important to the Comanche, was rich with clay and the residue of the past. We would come back.

The Tule Canyon site marks a crucial turning point in the history of the Comanche on the Southern Plains. As Lopez explained to Don Haragan, then Texas Tech president, "When I came to Texas Tech as a Visiting Scholar, I was curious about the university's relations with the Comanche, who once belonged to the part of the Llano Estacado on which the university now stands. When I learned that no such formal relations existed, it seemed to me that with the right kind of invitation, the Comanche could make a crucial contribution to education at Texas Tech. It wasn't until Bill Tydeman told me what had happened to the Comanche at Tule Canyon, however, that the outline of a ceremony began to take shape in my mind. On September 28, 1874, the attempt to kill the horses, to finally break the resistance especially of Comanche people, symbolized for me the near-fatal encounter between cultures on the Southern Plains in the nineteenth century. If we handle it properly, the events of that day, recalled in a healing ceremony, can affect both a rapprochement with, and a new and modern alliance with, the Comanche."

This Ceremony of Conciliation became a reality. The event and its historical background have been described by Texas novelist Henry Chappell in the September/October 2008 issue of *Orion*. Later, in a letter to Rory Suina, a reporter, photographer, and public information officer for the *Comanche Nation News*, Lopez described the evolution of the elements of the ceremony itself, an event that many regard as a signal event in relations between Native American peoples and institutions of higher education.

Dear Rory:

I am Texas Tech University's Visiting Distinguished Scholar. I work with the University's Southwest Collection on a variety of projects. When I first came to Tech, I wondered what kind of relationship the University might be maintaining with Comanche people. The link did not seem to me to be strong. Because the land the University sits on is land the Comanche once belonged to, I wanted to find some way to bring the Comanche people back into relationship with it. And I wanted students at the University to become better informed through an exposure to a Comanche way of knowing.

In reading Comanche history, I came across references to what happened to Comanche horses at Tule Canyon. This tragic event, of course, is not the whole story of the Red River War, and it is only a small part of the history of the Comanche people, but it spoke to me. I contacted the current land owner and received her permission to walk around in the canyon. The day I hiked there I found several very small pieces of bone and wondered whether these might be the bone of horses that were killed in the canyon on September [28], 1874. In thinking about this further, it occurred to me that if the University could recognize and acknowledge the nature of that tragedy, it would create a better understanding between the University and the Comanche Nation. And it occurred to me that some sort of ceremony which memorialized this part of Comanche history could be designed, that it would be possible to conduct a ceremony of reconciliation, with the help and permission of the Comanche people.

Some months after my first visit to Tule Canyon, I asked my friend Richard Rowland, a potter who lives at the mouth of the Columbia River in Oregon, if he would walk with me there. I hoped the canyon might teach us the right way to think about the killing of the horses. I couldn't really understand what I was looking for, but I knew that in the company of my friend and in a humble frame of mind, we might see something that neither man could see alone. When we visited the canyon in February, 2006, Richard and I scattered tobacco in the four directions and asked the spirits there to take pity on us and guide us to an understanding of what would be pleasing as a gift to the Comanche people.

We spent the day walking slowly and silently in the canyon. In the afternoon we felt strongly drawn to one particular area where we dug clay. Everywhere we walked that day we came upon the bones of coyote, deer, bobcat and other animals. They were emerging from the earth. They seemed to call out to us. We gathered them up carefully and put tobacco in the places where they had emerged. We packed the clay and the bones up and Richard carried them home with him to Oregon. Both Richard and I had had the same thought, that pouring water would be a central part of whatever the ceremony turned out to be. So Richard began designing a pot and a pitcher. While he was working on the designs, I took Texas Tech students out onto the Llano one day and gathered wood which we shipped back to Oregon. During the following year, Richard designed and fired several different types of pots and pitchers made from the clay from Tule Canyon and from the bones. He fired the vessels in a wood-burning kiln, and at the end of each firing he and I would look at the pots and the pitchers to see how well they represented the earth and animals of Tule Canyon.

For the final firing, Richard collected beaver sticks from the part of Oregon where he lives and I collected beaver sticks from the creeks around my home in Oregon and Harry Mithlo collected beaver sticks from Cache Creek on the Comanche reservation in Oklahoma. In June, 2007, Harry traveled to Astoria, Oregon, with Andy Wilkinson and on the last day of a seven-day firing, Harry and Andy fed the kiln fire with the beaver sticks and with the wood the students had collected. Seven days after the firing ended, Richard opened the kiln and he and I chose the four pots and four pitchers that seemed to be the right ones for the ceremony. These are the vessels we brought to Lawton, Oklahoma, to Comanche Nation tribal headquarters.

I was conscious, all the time I was trying to understand the nature of this ceremony, that I had no right to disturb the spirits in the Canyon. Still, I asked the spirits to guide us. I believed that if Richard and I acted in a humble manner and acknowledged our ignorance, the spirits would guide us in the right direction, they would show us a path that was respectful both of the canyon and of the Comanche people. That day we were in the canyon, I felt the horses were coming up out of the ground and saying, "Take us home, now. We want to go home."

In the ceremony at Lawton I wanted the clay vessels to symbolize a connection between two cultures. With the pouring of the water I wanted to symbolize a relationship between the University and the Comanche people. We share the water of the Llano, and if our children are going to do well, we have to take care of this water. It was chairman Coffey who saw the right way for the ceremony to conclude. He told the Comanche men who were holding the pots full of water to pour the water onto the ground.

It is my hope that the University will work closely with the Comanche Nation to provide all students at the University with a better education, and that by recognizing the injustice that occurred at Tule Canyon, the University could embark with the Comanche on a healing path.

Very best wishes,
Barry Lopez

The emotion of that ceremony stays with me. I still see the rapt attention of the Comanche women, their tears falling like soft autumn rain. I hear the beautiful words and recall the depth of the speeches. The sun backlit the horses in a pasture next to the ceremonial ground, their gaze transfixed on the ceremony.

Lopez shared a bit of his field methods with me after the ceremony concluded. Still fresh in his mind was his work at Tule Canyon prior to the ceremony. A corral of horses, milling nervously, was located at the top of the road leading into the canyon. As we descended into the canyon on that first visit, several people were close around us. Lopez told me, "If there weren't cameras and other people around, if I had some privacy, I would have been pushing, pushing, pushing, to make myself more vulnerable to this place. I'd have gone straight to the corral where the horses were, just be there with them. I'd have sat there on the corral fence, not looking for anything in particular. I wouldn't have had any questions in my mind. I'd just want to be present to the horses. And wait."

The Search for Seamless Coherence

Finn Rock, Oregon
April 29, 2002

WILLIAM E. TYDEMAN: *I was intrigued with what we were talking about earlier. You had a recent conversation where the speaker made the distinction between nature writing and the work of literature.*

BARRY LOPEZ: Well, I think the person was trying to offer a compliment, but the way it was phrased, I guess you might call it "revealing." He said his work was different from mine because he was "a nature writer but not a literary writer."

This isn't something I spend a lot of time trying to unravel, but for me, "nature writing" is a form of literature. I don't like the term itself because it suggests an emphasis on the metaphor. You wouldn't call a novel informed by an awareness of Freudian psychology "psychology writing," you'd just say it was a novel. Also, unfortunately, for many people "nature writing" means a narrow type of writing—nonfiction dealing with elements of the natural world and going no further. The body of work I identify as "nature writing" uses natural history, archaeology, anthropology, biology, and geography to explore themes that literature traditionally has addressed—justice, Eros, and so on. For example, what is the nature of a successful individual life considered against the fate of a community? What are the boundaries of a moral contract with the world? The central theme in nature writing, I think, is a question: What are just relations? What is a person's just relationship with a place? What are just relations between a community and a place? Today, these familiar questions are increasingly informed by biology. Biologists, as distinct from politicians, with their constituencies and agendas, are saying, "We have a problem here. We're going to be in a lethal crunch for fresh water in twenty-five years," or "We're now facing terrifying issues because of our inadvertent disturbance of viral ecologies." So I think what you can say now about nature writing, as it's developing, is that it's an attempt by men and women, who in another era might have written literature informed by other metaphors—social class, destiny—to address human biological fate. But I have to assume that people in the academy still strongly resist the whole idea that natural history can be an appropriate framework for literature.

TYDEMAN: *Well, that makes me think of the label applied to your nonfiction work—creative nonfiction.*

LOPEZ: I don't know what to say about these labels. I don't ponder them, you know. They don't arise from within me. They come from the outside. They're imposed. If somebody wants to call what I do "creative nonfiction" or "the fiction of fact"—a term applied to some of my short stories—it's none of my concern. From time to time in a specific interview or in reading a book review, I might be irritated with this, but it's no more than any writer's ordinary irritation with being put in a box. "Creative nonfiction" implies there's a kind of nonfiction that's not creative, and I don't know what that's supposed to be. If you tell me it's journalism, well, we already *have* that term. Journalism is not noncreative nonfiction. I think the term "creative nonfiction" came about in response to a body of work produced in the sixties that was not necessarily informed by the techniques of literary fiction, dialogue for example, but that was written with greater concern for the language itself. So "creative nonfiction," I think, became a term for the nonfiction of beautiful language, where the reader sensed the writer was as much interested in the language as the subject. For me, in both fiction and nonfiction, there's no separation between the intensity of my interest in the idea or subject and the intensity of my interest in expressing the idea well. My rewriting, I would say, is a struggle to find beautiful language, not so much a struggle with thoughts—although it's very difficult to take this apart.

"Thought" is not a word I associate with writing fiction. Writing fiction is not a kind of "thinking" for me, it's a kind of "expressing." Writing an essay is a kind of "thinking." Or let's say that in the essay the effort to think is more intentional—"now this thought is going to lead to this thought." In fiction, for me, the next scene grows more legitimately out of the emotion of an earlier scene, rather than out of any factual material. It is intuitive, not logical or expository. Plot is not something that has ever strongly attracted me. I'm not trying to write a literature in which there's some mechanism at work. I'm interested in something else that I can't actually name, but that compels the story I'm writing as much as plot compels the stories of other writers.

TYDEMAN: *So the connection you often see in fiction is between emotion and landscape, where in Arctic Dreams it was between imagination and landscape?*

LOPEZ: Yes. And although it's a very fine line of distinction, that's where I want to move next in nonfiction, to the relationship between emotion and landscape. And the single emotion I'm most interested in is hope. Hope is a virtue but it's also an emotion. It would be just as interesting, I think, to explore the relationship between the emotion of anger and landscape. Some of the things I'm curious about here are the ways in which the perception of volumes of space falls together with a sense of time passing, an emotional awareness of volume and increment. How, by bringing spatial volume and temporal increment together, can I create something that makes a reader hopeful? I think you can evoke aspects of the land in prose in a way that makes people hopeful about their lives. I think you can also describe landscapes that are not just physically but metaphysically dreary, and that those descriptions can make readers lose a sense of hope about the subtle possibilities of their own lives. For me—and maybe there is some mode of critical thinking about this—the creation of story is a social act. It's driven by individual vision, of course, but in the end I think story is social, and part of what makes it social is this impact it can have on the psyche of the reader. My sense is that story developed in parallel with the capacity to remember in *Homo sapiens*. I don't mean "where did we cache the food last spring?" but memory operating at a more esoteric level, recalling, say, the circumstances that induced loving behavior. Story, it seems to me, begins as a mnemonic device. It carries memory outside the brain and employs it in a social context. So you could say, a person hears a story and feels better; a person hears the story and they remember who they are, or who they want to become, or what it is that they mean. I think story is rooted in the same little piece of historical ground out of which the capacity to remember and the penchant to forget come.

TYDEMAN: *You have written a good deal about memory and the relationship of memory to story. But you've also said that we as humans aren't attuned to the vertical dimension. We tend to focus on the horizon— the plane that's in front of us. You suggested that between these spatial dimensions there is a possibility for new ways of seeing.*

LOPEZ: Or thinking. Artists and writers are constantly changing the sense of orthodoxy in perceived relationships—visual, acoustical, spatial, emotional relationships. All this work stimulates thinking. So, knowing we are horizontally oriented, it just makes me more curious about the vertical dimension. As a writer, I always want to stimulate a sense of awareness. I want to create and intensify patterns. When I listen to music, I always hear patterns.

When I'm walking in the woods, I sense patterns. Walking in the woods with somebody, I might identify a plant, but the naming of the plant comes out of a pattern of movement, the conjunction of a time of year with that particular space. For example, knowing that I'm coming off a ridge and down onto a south-facing slope in May, I'm going to be looking for certain kinds of plants that I'm not going to find on the north side. So I'm always looking for these patterns when I'm writing, though I'm not necessarily *thinking* about a pattern—it's like I've caught something in a sidelong glance and, like a painter, I'm trying to render it. I'm making a pattern in language that stands in place of the pattern that I've seen or felt. But this kind of intelligence can also get in the way of a story. I have to remind myself sometimes when I'm writing fiction that it's a good thing *not* to be thinking, because then I might be trying to make a point. Writing a short story to make a point seems vaguely contradictory to me. In fiction I don't want to make a point, I want to report a pattern I'm aware of, make it work in a dramatic narrative, and leave it at that, and trust that the reader encountering this pattern will be compelled to think about life differently.

Shifting temporal increment and spatial volume within a story is something I want to explore now. Take one extreme, "doing time" in prison, where the increments of time, for the most part, never change. From one day to the next it's a routine. And the spatial volumes never change. The nightmare of being in prison is that there is only this one spatiotemporal pattern, and it drives you *deep* into places you don't want to be. So to get out of prison, literally or figuratively, would be to stop "doing time," to break that pattern. I think it's legitimate to posit that many people in this country live the lives of prisoners, no matter how much money they have or how much freedom they think they've got—because they can't make or don't want any change in their spatial or temporal frameworks. Take this one step further and you're face-to-face with fundamentalism. Fundamentalism, for me, is the sign of a failure of imagination. It's the inability to modify spatial and temporal frameworks in the face of trouble, or an unwillingness to do so, or complacency about the frameworks you're using.

I think what stories do is change slightly the ordinary spatial and temporal frameworks of life, so that you can recover a feeling we often lose, a sense of the inexplicable weirdness of everyday life. Our imaginations are largely colonial, in the sense that we wonder how to control everything we can. If something resists us, we either find a way to control it, or as a last resort, believe we control it. The adolescent notion of controlling nature, for example, is an expression of this tendency to believe that human beings can control everything. I love this phrase, "controlling your emotions." It prompts the question, Why? If somebody said, "shape your emotions" or "reshape your emotions," I could understand that, but to "control" them is to take the fundamentalist's position that there is a right and a wrong way for emotion to express itself. Certainly, morally and legally there is a reason to control emotions like hate and anger, but to control your emotions means to some extent to give up the landscape in which your emotions are the principal explorers.

At this point in my working life—I'm sitting here at home on a spring afternoon in 2002—I know I'm after something that's been brewing for a while about memory and emotion in fiction and nonfiction. Whatever work lies immediately ahead of me now, it will address those questions. I feel a dividing line coming between previous work and work to come.

TYDEMAN: *I wonder about the notions of time implied in the temporal and spatial landscape you're talking about. Crow and Weasel is set in mythic time. Does the choice of mythic time for a story create a stronger emotional response on the part of the reader?*

LOPEZ: I think not stronger, but different, a different sense of where we are. we're in myth time, things have shifted to such a degree that we're no longer in what's called "ordinary reality." That means the possibilities for the characters are very different. If we're in myth time, trees are going to talk and no one's going to say, "This can't happen." For me, there's an elision here, though, between "ordinary reality" and "extraordinary reality." What some people call "magical realism" I understand as the extraordinary dimensions of ordinary life. In some cases, with some stories, what I'm trying to do is just that—draw a sense of the extraordinary from the context of the ordinary. It's often indirect. It comes out of word choice, syntax, and sentence rhythm. Suddenly there's a door where there's not been a door, and you walk through it.

TYDEMAN: *So the distinction between an analytic frame of mind—the thinking mind—and the imagination, it's not so much a conscious choice, but is it impelled or dictated by the structural requirements of the story?*

LOPEZ: Yes, I work in these forms called fiction and nonfiction. I have fairly conservative ideas about what the differences between them are, but what each form comes down to for me is a moral contract, an understanding between a reader and a writer. The writer's side of the contract says something like, in exchange for your attentiveness, I will make a dependable report about the kind of life we're sharing. If it's a work of fiction, you can depend on these characters being motivated by something in the story or in the history that precedes it. You're not going to feel, reading the story, that you've been "had" or get the sense that it's only about the author. So the story, I would say, has some requirements dictated by entering into a relationship with the reader; but for me as a writer, what's driving the whole thing is invention. Or imagination.

TYDEMAN: *But invention or imagination make use of devices that may never transgress into certain other forms of experimentation. In the arena you describe, are there limitations?*

LOPEZ: I'm having trouble with this because I feel like a writer who's been given two forms to work in by his culture, and who uses those forms, but sees them both as a means to an end. The end, for me, is always the same—maintaining a good relationship with the reader. I've used the distinction before between an "authentic" and an "inauthentic" story. What makes an authentic story, I would say, is establishing a moral relationship with the reader. The reader believes you can be trusted. If you asked me what makes a story inauthentic, it could be making up a personal history, for example, and offering it to the reader as nonfiction. In memoir, I don't think you should make up anything crucial or pivotal. Of course, in memoir both the reader and the writer know many details are lost and so substitutions are made. The issue is not the imperfection of memory but deceit. The idea of an imperfect memory strikes me, actually, as a misnomer. I don't understand memory as a mechanism pointed toward perfection, which records the world like a camera. Memory is the record of a process of *selection*. What an individual selects out of all that might be remembered in a moment grows out of that individual's personal history and emotional state. If you and I witness the same event and remember it differently, that's an expression of a difference in our personalities. In an ideal society, instead of asking who remembers what happened, we'd say, "Will everyone who saw what happened tell us what they remember?" That's what a library does. That's why there are so many books in the library.

My sense that story originated as a response to the development of complex memory is an idea that I can feel growing in me now. I don't know where it's going to take me; but I can say I'm not comfortable as a reader with the idea, for example, of a memoir that documents a life that was never lived. I think such deceptions are part of the burden of misdirection society has to deal with now, because it has banked so heavily—and so wrongly, I think—on the importance of the individual. If a society diminishes its people, it will intensify the need each person feels to be known. Advertising preys on that sense of insecurity. And the insecurity itself generates a society that becomes wayward and unstable.

I'm actually struggling with this now, because I think that there *are* rare people, singular people—a Bach, a Beethoven. You go back in Western history and pick out the really remarkable few. Jung said of Christ and Buddha that these men were their own idea—singular personalities. So I'm having trouble reconciling my belief in the primacy of community with a belief in the legitimacy of the extraordinary person. I prefer to understand extraordinary people as an expression of the community shaped by that individual's singular vision. I see their service to society as an ability to combine large- scale personal vision with an awareness of the plight or needs of others. For the writer— and this has nothing to do with genius and everything to do with an individual's artistic vision—maybe the great service is to fight against everything that destroys imagination.

TYDEMAN: *Individual talent and the imperative of modernism to "make it new" would imply that certain figures would consciously break with tradition in an attempt to establish their own artistic talent, their own genius that eschews any relationship to the past. Couldn't we argue that some artists throw away the past to create a form that is new and unique?*
LOPEZ: Well, "make it new." I think maybe the only people who have been successful at that are car salesmen. "Make it new" is the injunction to continually change the cosmetic facade of objects in order to stimulate their purchase. So even when something new is *not* substantially different, the expectation is there from advertising and sales and marketing people to pretend it is. The fantasy drives the compulsion. Perhaps what Pound meant by his admonition to make it new was that we must be reminded of the same things over and over because it is in our nature to forget. We create stories in order to defeat forgetfulness, and to get through to people in succeeding generations you have to make the story new. You have to tell the ancient story in a contemporary idiom. The idea of newness for its own sake is at the foundation of consumerism. It opens the door to a life of detachment—the affliction

of distraction. If life is actually always new, certain questions of faith, questions of allegiance become moot. But if you say, make what we already know more vivid or more apparent for a modem age, then yes.

These questions are extremely complex because what they require is that the writer *think* about what he or she is doing, and then express it. But, again that's not what writing is about, anymore than that is what painting is about. The occasional very articulate writer may be able to say something intellectually striking, but most of us just write. The writer's special skill is to see patterns and then make them come alive in words. But what we're actually up to, that's the province of critics.

TYDEMAN: *Are writers worth listening to when it comes to defining terms like "nature writing"?*

LOPEZ: I don't know. If you're angry because someone puts you in this box instead of that one, sure, you think about those terms. But to the extent you think about them, you've turned away from your real work, which is to be a storyteller. I don't think the job is any bigger than that for a writer—tell a story, that's what you say to yourself all the time. Stop thinking and tell a story. And remember that when you're telling the story, it has this social dimension. You've got to be aware of the reader, that relationship with the reader has to be a good one, and that means you can't lie.

TYDEMAN: *Lying. That's a provocative word.*

LOPEZ: Rather than say you can't lie, I'd say a writer should be careful with issues of authority. If I go to the Arctic and I watch a polar bear kill a ringed seal and I decide the event will be more memorable if I dramatize what was there, that means being selective with detail and the sequence of events. Some will be mentioned, others won't. So here's ten moments in the event with the polar bear. I select six, in sequence, to convey the event. For me, that falls within the realm of what's permissible. But if you go past that, if you describe things the bear didn't do, maybe to create a greater sense of danger or something like that, you're on dangerous ground. And if you actually insist that the bear did something that it didn't do, we're not in the realm of story anymore. We've moved into the realm of the imagination, which is fine as long as the reader knows that the ground here has shifted. As long as you're reporting what the bear did, the bear is the authority. When you start reporting what you imagine the bear did or could do, then the writer has become the authority for the event. When you ask the reader to accept the bear as the author of the event when it's you who is the author, you're lying to the reader.

TYDEMAN: *To shift examples here, doesn't a lot of confusion in American nature photography come from a disagreement over issues of authority?*
LOPEZ: If you present a photograph of something, even given the shortcomings of the technology, of the film and the camera, not to mention reducing three dimensions to two, our conventional agreement is that this is still pretty close to what I would have seen if I had been there. If two animals are doing something in that photograph I believe it happened, because the authority for it—by convention—is within the province of the actors, the animals. But if someone digitally removes one animal or adds other animals, the authority for the image lies with the manipulator of the image. And we need to be told that. Again, it's not one is right and the other is wrong. When you hand me a photograph of two elephants and you've digitally manipulated what one of the elephants is doing, what you're telling me is, "I'd like the authority traditionally granted in nature photography to the animal *also* to apply to my work of imagination," and that's dishonest. What you want is an integrity not your own.

To go back to the reader, what the reader is asking upon picking up a piece of work is: Where does the authority for this work originate, with the event itself [nonfiction] or with the author [fiction]? What are the rules going to be?

TYDEMAN: *The author as authority remains, however, a very complex issue.*
LOPEZ: In nonfiction the event being described is the real authority, but you can have a range of authoritative reports. In fiction, the author can do whatever is desired, starting with inventing the events. The tricky part is making the claim to authority. Some fiction is an insult to the reader's imagination because it's under the rigid control of a writer too enthralled with the authority of his own imagination.

CONVERSATIONS WITH BARRY LOPEZ

There's no room for the reader's imagination. A similar thing occurs in nonfiction, where a writer draws pedestrian conclusions from the material but assumes an authoritative voice. One of the reasons I love *Moby-Dick* is that you know in the first three words that by telling you to call him Ishmael, the narrator wants an intimacy with you and that there's going to be room for you in the story. That's very different from an opening line like, "I'll call you Jack." One signals the presence of a writer who wants to be the reader's companion, and the other the presence of a writer who intends to be the reader's authority. When a scientist writes for a technical journal, the authority for the report lies with the scientist. There's a call to be courteous, respectful of the reader's imagination, but the reader is saying, "You're the boss. I have no experience with this, only a limited knowledge to bring to bear. I'm trusting you to follow a formula, and then we'll see where you get." So in certain kinds of writing the authority has to lie with the writer, though I don't think of a scientist presenting the results of an experiment as a writer. I think of writers as artists, preparing engaging written reports on the meaning of life. That's too generalized a definition, I realize.

TYDEMAN: *But it's report writing.*
LOPEZ: The issue of writing ingenious prose aside—Joyce, for example—what most of us are doing as writers I think is trying to make patterns that excite and reassure the reader, and in that search we're aware of the reader's presence. A lot of writers I'm sure would disagree with that. They would say, no, I'm giving you the shape of my own imagination and you can take it or leave it. Or I'm telling you what I think, and you'd better listen, because I'm brilliant.

TYDEMAN: *"I write for myself and others, and the others, dear reader, are an afterthought."*
LOPEZ: Yes.

TYDEMAN: *I don't think we need to go too far with this, but you mentioned photography and the challenges in nature photography that come with digitization and issues of authority. The American writer Wright Morris for a period in his life experimented with combining photographs with his fiction. Morris and his critics decided eventually that the effort didn't work. The photo and the novel simply were not compatible forms. The photograph was a medium for fixing an image, while prose gave the imagination freer rein. Does that make sense to you? Did it have any bearing on the decision that you made early in your career to give up photography?*

LOPEZ: When I published *Desert Notes,* I included photographs that drew on some imagery in the stories and that I meant to set a kind of tone. I don't know if it was successful or not, but when *Desert Notes* came out in paperback, nobody argued for keeping the photographs. With *River Notes,* I made a series of photographs I intended to accompany the stories in the hardback edition, but I was discouraged from including them. That pretty much ended the idea of combining my fiction with my photography. They were not compatible, in the way you suggest. And then when I quit photographing altogether, two years after *River Notes* came out, the issue became moot.

I have combined my work with the images of other visual artists. I find it stimulating to write in the presence of someone else's images, partly because I'm actively breaking down an idea I'm not comfortable with, the idea of individual genius. I don't have an ensemble sensibility, I don't want to get together with other writers in a room and see what we come up with. But if a photographer I respect hands me a set of images and I react strongly, it can stimulate the desire to do something in parallel, in the belief that the reader and viewer will get something yet again larger than what either the writer or the photographer or painter might be able to do alone. .

TYDEMAN: *You've said that you never really thought very much about how a change of approach occurs in your work.*

LOPEZ: If I go back to *Of Wolves and Men,* I see some of the homework shining through. What I see with *Arctic Dreams,* eight years later, is an ability to more seamlessly incorporate research into a long narrative. An indication of the difference came for me when an editor who read *Of Wolves and Men* closely also read *Arctic Dreams* very closely and initially guessed they were the same length. *Arctic Dreams* is twice as long as *Of Wolves and Men.* And what that told me is I'd learned a lot about how to make something big, less cumbersome.

What I also see, comparing those two books, is my continuing interest in trying to combine visual elements with my prose. It's easier of course, in nonfiction. Still, in designing *Of Wolves and Men* I wanted to include photographs that had only a tangential connection to the accompanying prose, photographs that had no captions, photographs that worked more like charts, and so on. And then with *Arctic Dreams* I dropped photographs altogether, because this was a different kind of prose.

My fiction has also evolved. I don't want to get into the question of what *River Notes* and *Desert Notes* are as forms. That was the way I thought of story at the age of twenty-three, twenty-four, twenty-five. I was trying to search out how story worked for me. When I was first starting to make my living as a writer, I felt I had to take editorial direction in nonfiction. I had to make some compromises with the market in terms of what instinct was driving me to do. My fiction, on the other hand, wasn't something I imagined anybody would be commercially interested in. So, although I sent the stories out and was disappointed when they were returned, I didn't think, "Oh, I've got to find out what the most popular or acceptable short story forms are today and imitate them, and then I'll be published." I just went on writing the kind of stories I liked to write. The form I use in *Desert Notes* and *River Notes,* which some people call parable or "fact-based fiction" or "imaginative nonfiction" or even "essays," is simply fiction to me. To be asked to discuss or defend the form was a non sequitur. When *Winter Count* came out, I thought, okay, the interplay here of character, event, and setting is now recognizable as more or less traditional. The stories remain idiosyncratically my own, but I'm not going to have to listen to this "Is it fiction, is it nonfiction?" anymore. But by then, as one editor told me, I had "a considerable nonfiction persona to overcome." Adding to the confusion about my work was the fact that I was also at the time a landscape photographer.

····

I remember one day I presented my portfolio at National Geographic and the picture editor said, "I'd love to send you on assignment but

I can't, not until you start photographing people." He was saying, "You're a good landscape photographer, but this magazine is about people, too, and I see no evidence that you can do that." I was, to be sure, reluctant to test people's privacy, so I didn't carry through there. But I didn't have to. My bread and butter, my working life as a writer, was in nonfiction. (I was making part of my living as a landscape photographer then, and I continued to combine photography with my nonfiction, but I didn't take the necessary steps to become commercially or even artistically successful as a photographer. Photography remained a way for me to experiment.) It irritated me that my early fiction was rejected, but it didn't put me at a financial crossroads. I just turned away from fiction for a while. I also stopped photographing altogether in 1981.

Through the rest of the eighties I am writing essays and finishing the research for, and writing the early drafts of *Arctic Dreams,* which comes out in 1986. I don't know if any fiction is even published in the middle eighties. A collection of essays, *Crossing Open Ground,* comes out in 1988 and at that point I return to fiction. I write the first draft of *Crow and Weasel.* And what I recognize in *Crow and Weasel* is that for the first time I'm creating characters that are more complex than characters in my earlier stories. Their emotional lives aren't more complex, but their development is. There's a clearer arc of change than there has been in any short story. At 16,000 words, it's also the longest piece of fiction I've written.

So at that point I've finished a long decade with nonfiction and I'm back to writing fiction, in a form different from *Desert Notes* and *River Notes.* Also quite different from *Winter Count.* I continue to think about *Winter Count,* however, because I know that there's something going on in that book that I want to go back to. When *Field Notes* comes out in 1994, a set of stories all written between January and June of 1992, I have the feeling I've pushed that form from *Winter Count* further. *Field Notes,* even though it's promoted as the third book in a trilogy with *Desert Notes* and *River Notes,* actually has more to do with what was going on in *Winter Count,* thirteen years before. With *Field Notes* though, the trilogy is finished, and I no longer feel in a defensive frame of mind about what I was up to with *Desert Notes* and *River Notes.*

TYDEMAN: *Then comes* Light Action in the Caribbean.

LOPEZ: When *Light Action in the Caribbean* comes out in 2000, I feel settled as a short story writer. As we speak, I am nearly finished with another collection of stories. And I see more fiction coming, some of it large-scale I hope, and some of it in collaboration with a painter and visual artist named Alan Magee. My attention these days is divided around a large work of nonfiction, a collection of essays, and these several fiction projects.

The nonfiction book is a kind of emotional memoir called *Horizon.* For a while now the subtitle has been *The Autobiography of a Journey,* by which I mean a story told in the first person about what happened to me when I went somewhere. What I want to get to with *Horizon* is something within the scope of autobiography. For many years as a nonfiction writer I kept myself on the margins of my narratives. If you asked me why, I'd have said, "The reader may be attracted to the way I see the world, but the reader is not really interested in me, so I don't think I should be in the narrative." In other words, in the past I would rather the informing incidents occurred to someone else. But somewhere here in recent years that started to shift. I see two things happening now. One is, I'm not as inhibited as I once was about writing about myself. If there is a marker on a line that separates the personal from the private, I've moved that marker a little bit. I'm more willing to talk about what was once part of my private life. I don't mean my relationships with my friends or what remains my private life. I'm talking about making myself more open to the reader as a narrator. I see that happening, the development of a narrator in my nonfiction who is more vulnerable. But I also see something else. Over the past ten years I have become a more active thinker about culture. Ten years ago I would have insisted that I was only a writer. It would be dishonest of me now to say that I'm only a writer. I am actively engaged in thinking about where we are going as culture, engaged as a speaker, a conference convener, and a curriculum advisor.

TYDEMAN: *As a result, you're subject to a variety of labels.*

LOPEZ: I now see myself referred to as a philosopher, a public intellectual, a cultural thinker. It's hard to convey the combination of exasperation, discontent, and irritation I feel reading something like this, but it is false of me to disown it. For whatever reason—9/11 had a lot to do with it—I'm now much more active in ways that make people characterize you like this.

So I find myself changing at the same time the country is changing so profoundly. And I'm trying to see what to do. How to proceed.

Last year I wrote a piece for *LA Weekly,* "A Scary Abundance of Water," which, not to confuse the metaphors, was a watershed story for me. It's the frankest piece of autobiographical writing I've ever done. A friend of Stegner once told me that Stegner never would have written autobiography if he hadn't been able to find a way to situate his life historically and geographically in the narrative. If I can put myself in that company for a moment, I think "A Scary Abundance of Water" follows in the same path. The narrator of that piece—me—is saying, "I really don't see the point of writing about my troubled childhood unless it's historically and geographically situated. That's how I understand life. Human life has these strong historical and geographical components, and I'm going to set them forth strongly in this autobiographical piece, this memoir called 'A Scary Abundance of Water.'"

When you finish reading the piece, the historical and geographical elements reverberate in a different way than they did when you began, because about halfway in you encounter a blunt, unsentimental report of childhood sexual abuse. My intention in writing this piece was to handle this part of my private history in such a way that it wouldn't take over the story. It would get its due and no more. Childhood sexual trauma fractures many human lives. What I wanted in writing this piece was to contribute to a literature in which childhood sexual trauma—any kind of childhood trauma— was seen not as the organizing principle for an adult life but as a grievous offense that could sharpen a certain kind of awareness in an individual. It could help them isolate one layer in all the complex layers of water we call the ocean of life, and be able, perhaps, to report on it.

I haven't thought this out completely. I was asked to write that essay, that memoir, in 1994. I told the editor it was something I wanted to do, write about my childhood growing up in Southern California, but even as I told him that I knew I had no real interest in doing it unless

I was going to tackle what happened to me as a child. And in order to do that I needed a lot of help. I needed a lot of professional help, so I got that help and then I went into it, and I saw that my task was to disembowel my own trauma. This kind of violence overtakes many, many people. If you are a woman, you can say, "This happens to most of us." Knowing that's the case, the real question becomes: What can we do so it doesn't take over our lives? My answer is that story.

TYDEMAN: *Does this distort what you just said? Would it be incorrect to say what Borges said about his blindness, that each person must think of what happens to them in their life as a resource?*

LOPEZ: Yes. The trouble with that thought, though, is that some people who have been traumatized in their childhoods and who pick themselves up in the wake of those experiences and go on to lead what we would call a decent or productive life, develop, I think, lives with a fault line. Sooner or later, that fault line has to be attended to. So if you say, well, childhood sexual trauma is the writer's resource, you have to ask whether or not those experiences were attended to. Let's say that those incidents require a period of mourning or grief. In adulthood, recalling yourself as a child, you develop something like a parent-child relationship with yourself. You've got to be a parent to that damage; you've got to perform in a parental way toward that child, and part of what you go through is feeling grief and sadness and compassion. So I would say that the history that you have as a writer can be used as a resource, but you have to enter it emotionally; you can't just use it as an object. So if somebody said, "I can write effectively about rape because I was raped as child," my question would be, how have you dealt with your rape as a child? If you've gone into it and dealt with it, maybe you can write well about it. But if you haven't gone near it, you've essentially denied it as an emotional experience, and you're not going to write very well about it. In fact, you're going to perpetuate the system of denial that's kept you emotionally detached from those incidents in childhood.

My determination to explore that material in my childhood benefited me. But at this point, the only written works I can offer are two memoirs, "A Scary Abundance of Water" and "Madre de Dios." Where it goes from here, I don't know. I would say that I have a more mature sense of compassion and a greater tendency to reserve judgment after examining those years. And it's made me a different kind of writer.

TYDEMAN: *I'm not positing that there's a direct connection with what we've just been talking about. However, some reviews of* Light Action in the Caribbean *pointed out a darker vision in this collection. Several of the stories deal head on with the question of evil. You said to me once that you thought that as a writer you had developed a complex, more nuanced view, of evil. I'm not sure "nuanced" is the word I want.*

Lopez: Well, "nuanced" isn't a bad word. I'm just going to walk out on a limb here. If I fall off, let's start over. Ten years ago when I sat down to write, my thinking went something like this: reports of harm, cruelty, disaster, and evil come easily to hand in our culture. Trustworthy reports of kindness, ecstasy, and munificence, reports uncontaminated by sentimentality or any of a dozen sorts of neurosis, don't come readily to hand. It's much tougher to write a credible story that celebrates the good than it is to write a story that describes or indicts evil. My thought back then was that *all* of us have experienced harm, to a greater or lesser degree, and I'm going to assume the reader will bring that to the page, and regard me as a writer who, too, has had experiences of darkness. And I believed, because I was sexually traumatized over a period of years and was inside my parents' violent divorce, that I *had* seen bad things. But as my life went on, and as I saw, for example, starving children threatened by rogue soldiers in the Caprivi Strip in Namibia, I began to think I was kidding myself. I was living a life in which, in fact, in some fundamental way, I was emotionally detached. So I became interested—at first as an intellectual exercise—in writing a credible story about something unsettling. It occurred to me, also, that if I could structure a story collection in which my usual propensity for leaning into the light dominated, as usual, but insert in that arc of stories several pieces that were explicitly dark, I'd be doing something I hadn't done before. And then maybe somebody who couldn't quite accept my emphasis on the light, on the good in humanity, perhaps because they have been too heavily damaged to believe, could say that, at least on the page here, there's some awareness in this writer of what cruelty, what murderous behavior human beings are capable of, and I would have written a different kind of book.

I don't want to do the same thing over again as a writer. I remember after *Of Wolves and Men* came out, someone asked my agent in my presence what animal I was going to write about next. My agent said, "You don't understand him at all. He'll probably never write another book about an animal." I want to push into places I haven't been before. What happened with *Light Action in the Caribbean* was that in the early stages of exploring my own childhood sexual abuse, I just gave in to writing about unsettling events. I just went with the impulse to write these two dark stories, "The Deaf Girl" and the title story, "Light Action in the Caribbean." There is another story in that book, an earlier attempt, actually, to deal with material like this, but I think I have to explain something about it first. The short title is "Ruben Mendoza Vega." Before I wrote that story, I had always used narrators who were decent people. They may have been conflicted about something, they may have been maturing in some way, but they were always decent people. They operated out of a clear moral framework or maybe they were struggling to maintain that framework. This was one of the very few times I wrote a piece of fiction driven by a thought rather than an emotion. What I said to myself was, I wonder if I can write in the first-person voice of someone I don't like? That's where "Ruben Mendoza Vega" came from and, perhaps predictably, it's a mocking piece about a solipsistic imagination. Here's a man whose son has committed suicide right in front of him, figuratively. Not only does he not understand why his son killed himself, he's about to take over editing his son's journals and so kill him again by rewriting the journals to reflect what the father believes rather than what the son believes. I just thought of this, but Ruben Mendoza Vega's behavior toward his son—the quality of it, not the brutality of it—is not unlike what Corlis Benefideo is trying to save Phillip, the narrator of "The Mappist," from when Phillip goes back to his daughter. Corlis Benefideo is saying, "What you're trying to do is make your daughter like you." Of course, Ruben Mendoza Vega is never going to feel any bump there, because his son is dead. But Mendoza Vega is a self-referential isolate, an encrypted man, encrypted because of this elaborate code that he speaks in, the language of an imperious academic.

I don't know if I'll ever write another story as violent as "Light Action in the Caribbean," but I would also never say it's "something I got out of my system."

TYDEMAN: *Barry, could we carry this forward to the theme that runs through your work and that of your fellow writers attending your John Hay Award dinner, the unremitting attention to the dynamics of living in America at this time? You've commented previously about the mantle you've had to assume.*

LOPEZ: I would say that, as far as my assuming a "mantle" is concerned, it's not possible for me to assume such a responsibility. I think what I wanted to do in this weekend was explore some things that are very important to me as a writer. By asking us to discuss the literary and artistic response to terrorism, I'm asking for us to look at ourselves as writers and artists. Each of us is differently disturbed by myriad acts of modem terrorism. The pedophile, the suicide bomber, the ruthless entrepreneur. We have all these images of the terrorist. Should we feel a responsibility as writers and artists to craft something in response? Do acts of terrorism in our day and age have a special call on our talents? One of my responses would be that to respond to economic terrorism at this point in our history is an act of patriotism. And I think artists and writers in the United States do have a special obligation here.

Another reason that I wanted to explore the idea of a literary and artistic response to terrorism is that I don't like the separation people sometimes make between work that is called, and clearly seeks to be seen as, political, and work that is called apolitical or that is identified by its creators as apolitical. I'm not trying to be cute with semantics here. What I'm saying is that some writers and artists have a sensibility that allows them to be trenchant and cogent on political themes. Other men and women make far more esoteric, or allusive or indirect political observations, but these are just as legitimate. Some people respond quickly and vigorously, others are more comfortable working out their politics metaphorically, in a short story, for example. But to me they are both activists.

I wanted us to talk, too, about the various ways in which we behave as writers and artists with regard to terrorist issues. How do we transform personal politics into art and literature? How legitimate are group politics? That opens up the question of consensus and what propaganda is, and that opens up, I think, some very treacherous ground, the belief that you can "change society." I said over the weekend that probably the only thing we'll ever be able to do is eliminate some measure of unnecessary cruelty. But changing society—if you mean by changing society, creating a world of total peace, a world without war, we don't have any evidence that this is possible. We feel the need for it because, as the lethal nature of our weaponry accelerates and the number of guns in private hands proliferates, warfare has a more and more terrifying aspect. My interest really is in asking this group of people, whom I respect so much, to feel comfortable discussing the issues.

To jump sideways here for a moment, when I go to Utah State or DePaul to discuss the undergraduate major Ed Wilson and I designed for Texas Tech, some people assume I have something to sell. I say right away that I am not here to sell anything. If you want a program like this, I'm delighted to work with you. But if you need to be convinced, I'll probably just go home. I'm interested, of course, in promoting the idea that such a thing is possible, but if you want to know if this will work at your school, you need to call these people at Texas Tech and say, "Here's what we're thinking. What do you think of what we're doing?" Similarly, if somebody convenes a group of people to talk about the literary and artistic response to terrorism, the assumption is people will come up with an answer and they'll want to proselytize. But I'm just trying to induce good conversation. I feel compelled to do it because these are perilous times, and nothing I see suggests times are going to get better.

TYDEMAN: *At the same time, it also suggests that in symposia, or in the classroom, there may lie radical ways of reconfiguring the critical thinking and learning processes. We're coming not as experts, not with predefined ideas. We have only an intuition or a hesitant hint of an answer; but here we are, willing to engage in open-ended discussion about the implications and meaning of the crisis we face.*

Lopez: I agree and would emphasize that the reason I think of doing something like this is because I believe the writer and the artist have social responsibilities. I believe we have to consider these social responsibilities, just as much as we have to consider the integrity of our own artistic visions. My request to talk about the social and artistic response to terrorism is not a denial of individual politics or individual artistic vision. It's to emphasize that storytellers and artists have always been involved with determining the moral framework of the societies of which they are a part. I just wish we were more active in that area. Like many other people, I wish American writers were considered as candidates for ambassadorships, as South American writers are. In the United States ambassadors are either people being rewarded for political contributions or they are career State Department employees. Why don't American writers represent their country to a foreign nation? Historians suggest that it reflects the difference between the idea of literature in South America and the idea of literature in North America.

Tydeman: *Well, was it Octavio Paz who served in Mexico as ambassador in several different settings?*
Lopez: Yes. I think Neruda was also an ambassador.

Tydeman: *It's a very provocative point.*
Lopez: I've thought about this some with regard to Borges and Neruda. To say that Neruda was a socially conscious proponent of justice and a political man, and then to denigrate Borges as an academic, completely detached from the ruthlessness of certain people in power in Argentina, is too facile. For me, the politics of both men are legitimate, their expressions praiseworthy. Who is to say whether an acute sense of social justice is not just as stimulated in one segment of the population by Borges as it is in another by Neruda? If you believe in literature as a metaphorical exercise, you must accept that among all the complex layers literature can sustain, there will be some very powerful political layers, and I'm not talking only about *1984* or *Animal Farm*. Somebody could read a short story of mine or an essay of mine and feel their own politics stimulated or redirected or clarified. Does that mean I'm a political writer? No. It means I'm a writer. The moral, emotional, and aesthetic frameworks writers employ stimulate political thought.

TYDEMAN: *Is there is a connection here, too, with some of the Latin American writers whose work is infused with morality, spirituality, or a sense of God, as a creative force?*

LOPEZ: I think so, and the word I lean toward here is "divine," as in "a quest for the divine." I would say that as a writer I'm looking for divinity in the ordinary. And by that I don't mean solely what might be called "the presence of God." I feel a desire to identify and celebrate a numinous dimension of ordinary life, which as I keep saying is not ordinary for me. Part of the stimulation of living here where we're sitting now is that this is not ordinary—the voice of this place—to me. As soon as I am aware of this voice, the atmosphere becomes rarified, again. These trees, the movement of light on the river that I see through the trees. The birdsong in the wind is always rarified. My idea with "The Whaleboat" was that while reading a page I would look up and see this model whaleboat in a glass case in my workroom. Then I'd glance out the window, then look back to the page—ten seconds. If you want to experience the rarified imagery of that essay, stand right there where the kitchen table is and look out that window through those trees at the light on the water, and you'll see all of the layered imagery in that essay. So I'm after the numinous dimensions of this "ordinary" place. Those dimensions are connected with the divine for me because in them I see so many mutually informing metaphors. Cosmology's singularity, for example. The existence of a "something" that is there before space and time, that's seamless, that represents utter coherence, and we're aware that these words suggest what some mean by "God"—a seamless coherence, the collapse of all paradox.

When I hear geese pass over, they excite a sense of the vertical dimension of life here for me. It's just the few calls, but they're moving much higher in the volume of space we occupy together. That's what I mean about the ordinary—it opens directly into the extraordinary. What I'm after is how the numinous transits into the divine. I think "nature writing,"—that term I hate—is, some of it, a deliberate attempt to re-infuse the ordinary with the extraordinary, to re-infuse material life with spiritual life—to return metaphysics to physics. There are many different ways to say it.

TYDEMAN: *I'm going to read a short quotation from Wendell Berry: "Our fundamental mistake is that we have presumed to be authors of ourselves in our destinies, and that we have forgotten or denied we are a part of a great co-authorship in which we are collaborating with God and with nature in the making of ourselves and one another."*

LOPEZ: I like it. That's the way Wendell says it. A similar thought that I've had, a feeling I've tried to articulate on several occasions, is that the rift between Western culture and indigenous cultures comes about because indigenous people see themselves as still participating in Creation. Western culture sees itself as directing Creation. Indigenous people are satisfied to fully participate, Western culture wants to control. Indigenous people are wary of Western culture because its adherents become antic and angry when they're not in control. We condescend to indigenous cultures as the witless victims of fate. So I think what Wendell is saying is something close to that idea.

TYDEMAN: *To understand the nature of stewardship, the care for nature and the land, that exists within Western and Eastern traditions, does that hold out great promise for reinventing of American culture?*

LOPEZ: Oh, sure. Sure. And I think what we're talking about in the present moment, post 9/11, is the need for a constitutional convention. The reason for this is that we have a de facto fourth branch of government, American business, that has not been incorporated into the system of checks and balances that regulates the other branches of government. And business, more than government, now shapes life in the republic. I think we are also going to be compelled toward a reinvention of our culture simply because we are biological. In the past we've been able to say, with a certain amount of confidence, that we can do anything. What we're facing though, that we have not had to consider before, is that certain biological realities are transcendent. Without water, for example, we can't survive. Responsible scientists are saying there's not enough fresh water available to support a sanguine vision for humanity over the next fifty years. The water's just not there. What we're talking about here is an imperative. I think, again, that "nature writing" is a call to take seriously the responsibility here. A lot of what I'm saying, I realize just now, is set out in an essay of mine called "The

Naturalist." It didn't occur to me when I was writing it how revealing it was of my politics and my position, including my saying that the naturalist was situated today at the radical edge of any nation's politics. "The Naturalist" is saying that the biological possibilities for *Homo sapiens* dictate a change in the economic foundation of our culture.

TYDEMAN: *But when one thinks about changing the economic foundations, so much of what might be described as the agrarian tradition makes sense. It has a coherence; it has a pattern; it has meaning; but the cliché is, "There's no turning back." You can't take a culture that is hell-bent on industrial capitalism and transform it to where it may have been a hundred and fifty years prior. I wonder whether agrarian responsibilities and concerns, or a system of thinking that was based on stewardship and husbandry, can find a place in the twenty-first century.*

LOPEZ: Those are terms—husbandry and stewardship—that Wendell uses with a lot of power and intelligence. It's not a vocabulary that I'm very comfortable with, however, because it implies a proprietary relationship with the earth. If you say you're going to be a steward, it implies you have control over the fate of the things you steward.

TYDEMAN: *Through ownership, through property?*

LOPEZ: Through ownership or through property or through the assumption of a human authority imposed on the system. Species superiority, for example. The opposite of stewardship would be indifference I suppose, or detachment, and I wouldn't subscribe to that. If you say, "Would you care for this field, to ensure that the topsoil isn't washed away," I'd say, well, okay. But I'm looking for something else. If stewardship and indifference are on a continuum, I'm farther from that end where you don't care what happens to the field than I am from the steward who says, "It's my responsibility to be the caretaker here." I'm troubled by all this because if you claim to be the steward of a place, that's tantamount to believing if you don't do something it will be ruined. It won't be ruined, it will just record the impact that you've had on it as an indifferent occupant. There's a conceit here about human life that accepts, without examining the premise, that mankind—human beings—are the apex of creation, that they have this responsibility to be the stewards. Well, if consciousness is maladaptive, biologically speaking, and we end up overpopulating the earth, running out of food and water, and many or all of us dying, or if we create some kind of nuclear winter and lots of above- ground life dies, that's not the end as far as life on the planet is concerned. Sulfur-based life, not photosynthetic life, flourishes on the bottom of the ocean, and the mass of organisms living *below* the surface of the earth today is greater than the mass of organisms living *above* the surface of the earth. So, in evolutionary terms, you'd be scraping off life on the outside of the planet, not ending it by a failure of stewardship. Over hundreds of millions of years, from the sea vents and from surface environments under the skin of the earth; life would establish itself again among the minerals and nutrients on the surface of the earth. And off life would go, in some new direction. Evolutionary biologists tell us we'd never get human beings again. We'd get something else.

Stewardship is a very difficult thing for me to get at. I practice it. I encourage it. But I do not fully believe in it. A couple of weeks ago I was in Bethel on the lower Kuskokwim River. I was being escorted around town by a man named Oscar Alexi, a Yup'ik Eskimo man about my age, and he expressed despair about the fate of traditional Yup'ik beliefs. He said to me, "I wonder if we're just going to lose—that it will all die." And I replied, "Oscar, I think even if we were actually killed by people opposed to the whole idea of moral relations with the earth, you couldn't say that we'd lost." The idea is not that we lose, the idea is that this part of the gene pool, our part, is no longer selected for. It's selected against, and it disappears. Stewardship, for me, implies that the cards have been dealt in static time, and that humans hold all the aces. I mean, what are the obligations this evening of the steward deep in the interior of those parts of the Congo basin that aren't occupied by human beings? What's the role of the steward in the ecology of the *Ebola* virus? These things don't operate in a framework in which stewardship is the right word. A different concept, one that I would be more comfortable with, is responsible participation, in the sense that Aboriginal peoples mean participation. You could say that all animals participate in the world. But what culture and consciousness combine to give human beings is this concept of the responsible behavior of a participant.

TYDEMAN: *There's responsible participation . . . . In some of your earlier essays you said that as a young person struggling to find your way as a writer, the central question was, how can I be of service?*
LOPEZ: Yes. How can I help.

TYDEMAN: *I don't think that's changed.*
LOPEZ: No, it hasn't changed at all. It's a more informed sense now. I think even more deeply felt than it has been in previous years. Among the complications I feel around that issue now, are, if the idea for the writer is to serve, what happens to the writer's family? What part of the family do you deny in order to be in service to the community? The answer to that changes over time, but it's a question that you have to address, more or less every day.

Another question revolves around the concept of biodiversity. Biodiversity, it so happens, is a characteristic of life, but more importantly it's a condition *necessary* for life. The life that surrounds us, in other words, is diverse, but if it weren't, life wouldn't become boring, it would be over. So if you ask yourself as a writer, "How can I serve my people? How can I help?" You have to believe that it is through the cultivation of your own voice, a voice different from your neighbor's. Society benefits most from a diversity of voices when the speakers or the writers have taken great pains to be clear about what they mean. This is one reason I talk so often about education. I tend to say two things about university education. One is that the primary responsibility of the student is to learn to become discerning, to see the nuances in a situation, and to cultivate that frame of mind that prepares you to always look for the nuances. And to be discriminating, to be able to take two things that look alike and separate them. But the obligation in higher education for teachers is to provide for students in such a way that they can, first, understand what they mean, and then say it. So a student who is a math major and a student who is an English major face the same problem. Working with the large-scale metaphors of language and numbers, they set out to discover what it is that they mean, different from what the man or woman sitting next to them in the classroom means. And the responsibility of the teacher is to create a classroom where individual meaning can come to the fore. A protected environment. Students can make mistakes here without having to pay an inordinate price. The ability to say clearly what you mean—that's where the teacher's judgment comes in. "Within the context of this material," the teacher says, "I agree that you have something to say, and that it fits well within the discipline of English, or math, that it's a disciplined saying of what you mean. And I get it. I get what you mean. You have said what you mean well."

So, again, this issue of service to humanity. It means the writer has a special responsibility when writing an essay—to say this unique meaning, to say it beautifully. You can take this a step further and ask, what is the nature of the relationship between the writer and the reader? I would say that it's reciprocal, contractual, and moral. In the give and take of the gift cultures, if you're going to ask that your gift be the reader's time, then you have to give the reader something that's worthy of that time. The exchange has to be equal. You can't just say, I'm so-and-so, Ph.D., or I'm otherwise special, therefore listen to what I have to say. If you ask for the person's time, you have to write an engaging line of prose.

A four-year-old Barry Brennan with his mother (*third from left*),
northern California, 1949.

Barry Lopez and his grandson at the U.S.S. *Arizona* memorial,
Pearl Harbor, April 2012.

Mary, Barry, and Dennis Brennan in Southern California, 1951.

Barry Lopez, graduation portrait, Loyola High School, 1962.

Barry Lopez and his brother Dennis, Sacré Coeur,
Paris, August 1962.

Barry at the Cliffs of Moher, Ireland, August 1962.
Photo by Dennis Lopez.

Barry Lopez with biologist Robert Stephenson and sedated eight-year-old female wolf, Susitna River drainage, Nelchina Basin, Alaska, March 1976.
Photo by Craig Lofstedt.

Anaktuvuk Pass, Brooks Range, Alaska, June 1979.
Photo by Robert Stephenson.

Undisturbed Anasazi storage room, North Rim of the Grand Canyon,
above the Colorado River, February 1983.
Photo by Robert Euler.

A wounded hippo that had attacked Lopez's party charges him on the upper
Boro River, northern Botswana, May 1987.
Photo by Michele Stemp and Margaret Stemp.

Practicing crevasse rescue, Ross Island, Antarctica,
austral summer, 1988.

Barry Lopez in sterile clothes with Al Gore at an ice core drilling site.
Newall Glacier, Transantarctic Mountains, Southern Victoria Land, Antarctica,
November 1988.

Camped on the Polar Plateau, twenty kilometers from the South Pole,
November 1988.

Barry Lopez (*left*) and Tony Beasley (*right*), scuba diving, Galápagos Islands,
March 1991.

Edward Abbey memorial service, near Moab, Utah, May 1989.

Barry Lopez and artist Alan Magee, Dragon Cement Plant,
Thomaston, Maine, October 12, 2002.
Photograph © 2002 Monika Magee.

Barry Lopez and cellist David Darling, Erie, Colorado, April 1981.
Photo by Judy Houlihan.

Barry Lopez and author Jim Harrison, Wilson, Wyoming, May 1991.

Barry Lopez and his wife, Debra Gwartney, with their grandchildren
at the couple's home in Oregon, 2011.

Science, the Imagination, and the Collaborative Search for Form

Texas Tech University, Lubbock, Texas
March 6, 2004

WILLIAM E. TYDEMAN: *Barry, we talked about addressing these distinctions between fiction and nonfiction, and specifically about creative nonfiction or, as you prefer, literary nonfiction.*
BARRY LOPEZ: Well, this is a debate I really don't want to be in the foreground of. It puts you in the wrong frame of mind as a writer, thinking you need to shape your creative work to a category. When I was growing up, the only categories we dealt with were fiction, nonfiction, and poetry. I understood, fairly early on, I think, I had no gift for poetry. It wasn't a form in which I could express myself very well, and I had a flawed sense of concision. I could write a series of image-rich lines, and I understood something about music; but it was always narratively driven. So, fiction and nonfiction were my only forms. One thought I've had about nonfiction is that my generation of writers, people in high school in the late fifties or early sixties, experienced something perhaps unprecedented in American education—a major change in the curriculum because Sputnik went up. The space race. In the early fifties, you could've gotten into a very good college without a science background. My generation was the first to experience a *required* infusion of mathematics, chemistry, and physics before college. Some people destined to be writers and artists—people with a less literal, more metaphorical cast of mind—were profoundly stimulated by some of these large-scale tropes in particle physics, and by ideas like "approaching the limit" in calculus. These tropes were so

interesting, so suggestive to people like me, that when I entered Notre Dame, at the age of seventeen, I declared aeronautical engineering as my major. It took me a semester to understand that I really wasn't an engineer. What I was enthralled with were the metaphors of flight. And I couldn't have been the only "humanities major" who had this experience, of being drawn to the metaphorical richness of science but seeing that my work lay elsewhere. I became one of those writers who used the tropes of science nearly as often as I used metaphors from the humanities—from history and anthropology and the theater—to try to clarify what I meant. So, as my literary work developed, I don't think I felt compelled to steer clear of nonfiction. I didn't see nonfiction as a potentially limiting or lesser form. What I saw was that you could explore ideas like prejudice or dignity by focusing on the field methods of biologists.

TYDEMAN: *This exploration of the boundaries of form begins early in your writing.*

LOPEZ: When I was nineteen or twenty I began to experiment, as I understood it then, with fiction, to bend the classic pattern of a short story. That's where *Desert Notes* came from. But I wasn't compelled to experiment with the dichotomy between fiction and nonfiction. I don't think I actually understood this at the time, but what I was really attracted to was how the authority of fact could augment the authority of the imagination in writing fiction. What was occurring—and what I would later oppose—was the reverse: inventing "factual" material to enhance the impact of a piece of nonfiction. As I grew older, I began to encounter writers who felt comfortable making up things about their own experiences, their travel, say, and then promoting it as nonfiction—writing a memoir, in other words, about a life that never occurred. I took umbrage at that, I felt it was a con. That kind of work is more about the writer than the material. And it's at this point, for me, that the ethical relationship between writer and reader starts to break down. It seems to me you've got to have an ethical relationship with the reader. The reader needs to know how to get oriented around the material. What's the authority here? If what you're telling me is something you've made up, my imagination is going to engage in a fundamentally different way than it would if you told me this was something you were reporting—facts outside your control, facts I could verify. If you were presenting nonfiction about the Vietnam war, and I had the energy and the diligence to track down the names and the dates, the documents, and felt you were interpreting these in a way I wouldn't, well, that's okay. I can disagree. The important thing is, you didn't make it up. The piece is based on material I can verify. Of course, minor factual errors might abound, but that's not the issue. The issue is how you're courting my trust.

So that question, what's fiction and what's nonfiction, was never a question for me. They were fundamentally different, and I approached them differently as a writer. Either I was selecting factual material and using my imagination to share a plausible narrative—my "take"—or I was imagining the story, facts and all, in its entirety. In the former, authority lies mostly with the material, and the technique of presentation is the work of the imagination. With the latter, authority lies mostly with the imagination. For a piece of nonfiction, back then and now, I do a lot of library work. I conduct interviews and arrange to get some experience in the field. For a work of fiction, I just sit down at the typewriter. A different kind of preparation. It's rare for me to do *any* kind of research for a piece of fiction. One of the few times I did was with a story called "The Letters of Heaven," which I guess you'd call historical fiction because it's based on historical characters and it has a historical setting. I had to go to the library to make sure the story, set in Lima, was grounded in historical fact.

The problem for me, personally, around all of this—fiction and nonfiction—came with the publication of *Desert Notes*. I thought of *Desert Notes* as a kind of experimental book. I'd hoped, you know, for some welcome for the pieces in literary journals, but that wasn't why I was writing the book. I was writing it because I wanted to express the sensation of being fully present in playa deserts, and this is how it came out. I think I was about twenty-four when I wrote *Desert Notes*, so that's thirty-five years ago. It's hard to go that far back without colonizing the past, as I sometimes warn myself, without turning the past into what you wished it'd been, so it makes logical sense against the future. But I know when Jim Andrews—he published some of my first work in a magazine called *Ave Maria,* in the mid-sixties—when I went to Jim at Andrews McMeel, his publishing company, and showed him a manuscript I thought more worthy of his attention, *Giving Birth to Thunder,* he asked what else I was writing. I told him I'd written a book called *Desert Notes,* but I didn't think there would be any commercial interest in it. "Let me take a look," he said. So I sent it. He called me immediately and said he liked the book very much. "You're not going to understand this right away," he told me, "but even though you wrote *Giving Birth to Thunder* first and then *Desert Notes,* I want to publish them in the reverse order. The book you want to come out first," he said, "is *Desert Notes,* that's how you want to make a mark." So I said, "Well, okay."

It never came up in any discussion with Jim whether *Desert Notes* was a work of fiction. For some reason—and here, I guess, is a bit of the strangeness of life—I assumed that everybody understood that these first-person narrators I was using weren't me. But that's not how Jim and others understood it. When they went to the Library of Congress for cataloging information, they represented the book as a collection of essays. I wasn't aware of any of this until *Desert Notes* was published and I saw the copyright page. I called Jim up and I said, "This is a big mistake. This is not about me, it's about what these people who are *telling* these stories are imagining." Well, he apologized, but I don't really know what he was thinking. Possibly he thought the book was an easier sell as a work of nonfiction. And he did a couple of things—or let's say he allowed a couple of things to happen—that really angered me, one of which was to promote me as some kind of personality along with being a writer. That perception, unfortunately, stuck and got perpetuated. The kinds of things I wanted to do as a writer—to follow people into remote areas, on trips that might be physically demanding and difficult—those trips weren't about me, as I saw it. They amounted to serving an apprenticeship, about becoming grounded in an empirical life in order to write reliable nonfiction, particularly for a reader who couldn't or wouldn't go through such experiences. But from the publication of *Desert Notes* on, because, in the eyes of some magazine publishers and book publishers, I lived out there in the hinterlands [rural

Oregon] and traveled to these remote places and wrote nonfiction, I had some trouble being understood as a writer, as someone interested in language and ideas, and in fiction, interested in how factual material of a certain sort could enhance the authority of the prose. Instead—well, who knows how I was seen at *Harper's* [*Magazine*] and *Outside* and *GEO*, really. But I felt uncomfortable, being taken for an adventurer. And so, as that aura built up around my life, without my cooperation and initially without my knowledge, I felt placed in this category Andrews McMeel had created. So when they published *River Notes* it was published as a work of fiction, and I thought the business was settled. But, in between *Desert Notes* and *River Notes*, *Of Wolves and Men* came out. It threw a spotlight on me as a writer, and I resented being perceived as some kind of wolf advocate or outdoor expert and categorized so strongly as a nonfiction writer. Because of those perceptions, some reviewers of *River Notes* strained themselves trying to critique the book as nonfiction "philosophy," and some reviewers called it self-indulgent. Well, it wasn't about me. It was about the life going on around me in rural western Oregon, told by several different narrators using the first person.

I frequently use the first person in fiction because it allows for a kind of intimacy I can't get in the second or third person. Russell Banks said to me once, "I wonder if people really understand these nineteenth-century narrators of yours." And I said, "What do you mean?" He said, "If you're using the first person in fiction today, people assume it's somehow about you, but none of your narrators is like this." He meant they were creations, people with a point of view I stayed with as the story unfolded. It's a mistake to assume their views are actually mine, or that all these people can be subsumed in one consciousness. I know I'm on really tricky ground here, so let me say two things before I go any further. The commonest, lifelong resentment of every writer I know, no matter how successful they are in conventional terms, is that they are underappreciated or misperceived. So, I am complaining here about reviewers who took me for an adventurer as well as a writer and helped create something I felt I was up against in those early years. Second, I am obviously denying an essential part of my own nature here—I love being in remote places with people who really know what they're doing. What separates me from other "adventurers" is two things. My skills are not as honed as the skills of the people I travel with, and my primary intent, night and day, is to view what's happening as a story.

So, while I know most people don't make a mistake and call *Desert Notes* nonfiction, there are some other issues here that need to be addressed. (And I have to say, before I offend some intelligences I respect, that I can understand *Desert Notes* as experimental nonfiction. It's just that this wasn't my intent, for what that's worth.) *Desert Notes* came out at the same time there was a debate over Carlos Castaneda's books. Were these works of fiction or nonfiction? That debate had nothing to do with me, but it shaped some of the discussion about fiction and nonfiction and, for my generation, also discussion about the authenticity of such writing and the ethical questions it raised. I was one of the young, peripheral writers whose name came up in that argument who didn't want to be there. It was nearly impossible at that time for a creative person to be part of a community where drugs *weren't* readily available. My choice was not to take that step, so I became incensed when, on hearsay or after a quick read, people assumed *Desert Notes* was the fictionalized nonfiction of somebody who was experimenting with drugs. It irritated me because it undermined the authenticity and precision of my own imagination. Implicit in this argument was the idea that, on its own, imagination wasn't enough. I really didn't care what others were doing, but I had two reasons not to experiment. First, I had a history of traumatic sexual abuse. I didn't want to risk having it balloon and then compromise the tenderness I felt toward the world. Second, my experience with the physical world was sometimes so vivid I broke down in tears. I couldn't manage, I thought, a greater vividness.

I believed I was through with all this fiction/nonfiction confusion over *Desert Notes* and *River Notes* until Avon, my paperback publisher back then, without my knowledge, changed the marketing behind their paperback versions of both books and labeled them nonfiction. When my agent confronted them, they said that *Of Wolves and Men* and *Arctic Dreams* had had such a commercial impact, they thought the sales of *Desert Notes* and *River Notes* might be better if they were reclassified and marketed in this emerging genre of first-person commentary about nature. We forced them to repackage the books, but the fact that they had done this only added to the problem.

····

You can't do anything about the way your work gets interpreted. I've no recourse if people go back and look at some of my early magazine work, about tree falling and backpacking and such, and assume this is a full expression of what I was trying to do as a writer. I did that work carefully and well. It's how I made ends meet as a freelance writer. But, like many other writers in or out of an MFA program, I was sending fiction to literary magazines and hoping the stories would measure up. (Literary magazines didn't pay well, so the nonfiction work, my bread and butter, went elsewhere.) The early acceptance of my photos and essays by Robley Wilson at *The North American Review* was enormously important in shaping how I perceived myself as a writer. Some of the literary writers I met around this time, in my mid-twenties—Bill Stafford, Ursula Le Guin, William Pitt Root—basically said to me, "Even though you're supporting yourself by writing for *Popular Science* and *Popular Mechanics*, you're still one of us." When I was twenty-three and twenty-four that meant a lot, because I had just left the MFA program at the University of Oregon, after a single semester, and after that I got a very cold shoulder from them.

So, I don't know what to say about fiction and nonfiction now, all these years later, except that it's important for to me to state that *Desert Notes* and *River Notes* were early experiments for me in how people experience the relationship between themselves and a place outside their immediate control. I'd like to think that I could go back and say, "Here, in *River Notes* and *Desert Notes,* are the adumbrations of later work about the meeting ground between human life narrowly understood and life coming to us from the other side." I've had these feelings since childhood, that there was something on the other side, that nature was animated in a way Western culture rejected. Nobody ever disabused me of the idea, not even as a student in aeronautical engineering. When I left Notre Dame, I still believed strongly in the nonrational foundation, the spiritual dimension, if you will, of the physical world we call "nature." And when I became acquainted with

Native American metaphysics, with the huge range of other North American epistemologies, I thought, "Here are people who approach this the way I do, and I'm going to be comfortable if I look into this." So at this point, I don't think I was even focused on the differences between fiction and nonfiction. I guess we're in a paradox here. What I mean is, I'm always looking for ground against which to exercise my consciousness. I work in these fiction and nonfiction forms without thinking I have to make clear what the differences are. An encounter with Navajo epistemology, in other words, fulfilling that desire, is what drives the writing, whatever the form. I am after the experience first. Later, I follow the rules, as I see it, that the two forms impose in trying to tell the story of that experience. The major differences I see are almost pedestrian. If I've written a piece of nonfiction, I haven't made anything up. The basis for the work is factual truth. In fiction, outside of a piece of historical fiction, it's virtually all made up. The work rests, instead, on emotional truth. It's unusual for me to create a character modeled on someone I know, or even to create composite characters. On the other hand, you can go through my fiction and find characters showing up with different names and different attributes over the years, but who have a nearly identical spiritual bearing or essence.

TYDEMAN: *In* Light Action, *for example, some critics suggest that there is an intention—a conscious choice on your part to play with the boundaries, the borders, between fiction and nonfiction. What I hear you saying is that's not an intellectual exercise or game that you've chosen.*

LOPEZ: I have no interest in playing a literary game. Suggesting somebody's interested in "playing" with these boundaries is tantamount to saying they're more interested in an academic question than writing. If I draft a story, and the story comes up through successive drafts, and after it's finished a critic says, "This is interesting because, from the very start, this story is unfolding on the boundary between fiction and nonfiction," I'll say, "Okay." I'll be intrigued. But I have neither the critic's expertise nor the desire to pursue those kinds of questions. It's not why I wrote the story.

TYDEMAN: *Yes. Just to clarify a point, jumping back to something you said at the beginning, when you went to Notre Dame as an aeronautical engineer, you came to understand that your interest was in the metaphors of flight.*
LOPEZ: Right.

TYDEMAN: *Could you expand on that a little more?*
LOPEZ: Well, you know I talked about this a little bit in an essay called "Flight," about my raising pigeons when I was a kid, and my curiosity about the loss of the third dimension in modern life. We live now in front of these computer screens, in front of television screens and cinema screens and Blackberry screens. A lot of our experience comes from information gathered from only two dimensions. When I was a kid watching my tumbler pigeons falling and flying through all three dimensions, I found the experience exhilarating; and many years later when I began scuba diving, I found the experience exhilarating again— moving in all three dimensions. When I was traveling in the Arctic, the people I traveled with were always reminding me to get out of the flat-screen world I was unconsciously still in, the world most of us in Western culture live by. They were always reminding me when we were going somewhere to *turn around*, look at where we'd come from. Or to *look up*, to keep opening up this two-dimensional landscape in which I was navigating. The reason I chose to become an aeronautical engineer, I think, was my fascination with how the intellect and the hand come together. A lot of the characters in my stories are men who work with their hands but who also have a rich intellectual life, or they have a rich spiritual life and are engaged in some sort of manual labor. Aeronautical engineering, in my young man's imagination, was a field of study where the stream of informing ideas went back to Icarus, for example, to a desire to achieve a union with the divine through flight. Those kinds of possibilities—birds soaring and diving, a spiritual quest, exotic metallurgy—filled my daydreams. Aeronautical engineering seemed to offer a way with wind tunnels and model planes and other kinds of hands-on experience to join ideas of pure flight, and a haunting mathematics like calculus, to a world of materials. . . . .Well, it was combining the intellect and the work of the hand. In chemistry, you know, you have a

similar situation with laboratory experiments; but in aeronautical engineering you can take these ideas compelled by the story of Icarus, say, describe some of them in mathematical equations for laminar flow or lift, and produce a small-scale object and put it in a wind tunnel and see whether or not what you imagine will actually fly. You can go to an airstrip and actually fly the thing, actually fly an idea.

You know, it just occurs to me now, maybe in terms of fiction and nonfiction, that that's where those two worlds meet for me. I've got this desire to be absolutely accurate in the working out of the equations and a reification of the ideas, and at the same time I feel no boundaries in working with the raw ideas. You know, this is a funny thing that just occurs to me. Every writer, every creative person I know, whatever they do, has some aphorism or other pinned up around the desk. One that's been pinned up at my desk for many years is a postcard that shows two cowboys on horseback moving through white space. It's a kind of Andy Warhol image, stylized, all black and pink. The cowboys are speaking French, with the English translation in a set of word balloons. The perspective is looking up from below at these two cowboys, staring off in different directions, with the horses' heads in the foreground. The question one of them has asked his friend is, "What's your scene, man?" The other guy says, "Reification." And the first guy says, "Whoa, that sounds like big library tables and lots of books and piles of paper." And the second cowboy says, "Nope, mostly I just drift." Writing for me is often this kind of drifting through undefined space toward a story, toward reification.

I haven't thought much before about why aeronautical engineering was so attractive to me. But I'd have to guess that it offers the opportunity to combine these two forms of work, both of which I feel comfortable with—imagination and reification. I remember a review of *Winter Count* in the *Los Angeles Times* in which the reviewer said that most writers make either fiction or nonfiction their territory and that I seemed to have made the middle ground my territory, but to have done so without breaking faith with either form. She was saying that in *Winter Count* I was not breaking faith with fiction, but that the fiction was so informed by the *aura* of nonfiction that it brought nonfiction to mind. You hear a lot about bringing the techniques of fiction to nonfiction. I don't think you hear as much about bringing the techniques of nonfiction to fiction, but I can't be alone in trying to do this.

TYDEMAN: *That's true.*

LOPEZ: One of the reasons I'm aware of the different realms of fiction and nonfiction these days is that it serves commerce, but not society, to blur this distinction. In my work I want the difference to be clear, but I don't want to be confined by the forms. Someone who just picks up a story of mine—I can see why they might assume, just plunging into it, that it's nonfiction, because of my predilection to use the authority of fact to drive the story. So, I guess I have to accept some responsibility here, for people who are confused. But my feeling would be that after a few minutes the reader has to be paying enough attention to see what's going on. I can't set up road signs.

TYDEMAN: *Right. Was Whitehead's* work important to you early on?*

LOPEZ: Oh, yes. In fact, Whitehead's philosophy was the trigger for *Of Wolves and Men*. When I heard there were wolves in captivity at the University of Oregon in 1973, I wanted to go and see what that was all about, but I didn't right away. It was probably a year later that I visited the facility. The guy who ran that research program, John Fentress, had a double appointment in the Department of Psychology and the Department of Biology. I had a couple of long talks with him and learned he was an Alfred North Whitehead . . . you wouldn't call him an Alfred North Whitehead scholar, but he had more than a passing interest in Whitehead's ideas about the integration of matter, the metaphysics of ecology, I guess you could say. It was the tenor of those conversations with John and our mutual interest in Whitehead's ideas that made me think, when I was looking out the windows of John's office, watching wolves moving through tall grass in the pens out there, a short distance from the building, it was then that I thought, "I want to do something with this." That's remarkable intuition on your part, Bill. Yes,

---

*Alfred North Whitehead, 1861–1947, an eminent American mathematician, logician, educator, philosopher. Among his many influential ideas is that civilization consists of five fundamental ideals: truth, beauty, art, adventure, and peace.

Whitehead was the intellectual trigger behind wanting to write about wolves. I shouldn't say exclusively. There was a lot on my mind at that time about animals. I was, in some part of my imagination, looking for the form, the container for all of this feeling. My conversation about Alfred North Whitehead with John Fentress, that's where *Of Wolves and Men* came from.

TYDEMAN: *I see. You have spoken and written about your strong conviction that animals represent a parallel culture. From an early age you thought about animals and their world. You mention the pigeons and the relationship to flight that we've just talked about. Were you a kid that had dogs and cats . . . ?*
LOPEZ: Yes.

TYDEMAN: *. . . and pets of every kind?*
LOPEZ: No cats, just dogs. There's a piece in *About This Life* where I talk about the death of a dog named Kerry, a Kerry Blue Terrier. He was my first dog, and I've had dogs—I was going to say I've had dogs ever since, but I lost a dog in 1994 and haven't gone back to that place where I have a dog with me. My childhood, though, was a version of "A Boy and His Dog," wandering the countryside with my dog. I don't think I ever had any other pets but dogs, a turtle or something like that. When I was about ten, a friend of mine and I started catching alligator lizards. We built an enclosure to keep them in, but I don't know if we lost interest or we began feeling guilt, or what, but we turned them all loose after a while.

TYDEMAN: *You weren't out setting traps and . . .*
LOPEZ: No, we caught them bare-handed. You know, when you write a memoir, I suppose you try to tidy things up by eliminating episodes that don't reflect well on you. I've written a little in the memoir form, but I've also avoided writing about some things. Now that there's a bibliography of my work out, somebody could go back and look at what I've written about my life and put it together with what came later. But I don't have any . . . when I go back and look at my own life, I, too, become fascinated by the timing of these encounters, like the one

with Fentress, and how they generated the life I've ended up living. "A Scary Abundance of Water" is my only attempt to go back and make sense on paper, for strangers really, a period of long-term sexual abuse which I know helped shape my response to the world. When I looked at that material—and there are some other parts of my life I've never written about that would be as hard to address—I guess I've always known that I was going to have to *wait* a while. I don't want to write about something like this until I see a way to contain it, so it doesn't become more than it is. The only exercise in this regard I have to offer now is "A Scary Abundance of Water." But I have a kind of fascination now with the unfolding of my own life, not because I think I am more important than the next fellow, but because it's been a habit with me to keep track of things. I contain, for whatever it may be worth, a certain measure of what is distinctive about my generation; and if I keep track of those things, I can disappear but that record will still be there, some kind of spine to make sense of a time of unprecedented change. From Sputnik to email syntax, you know. A pedestrian example would be my working at a typewriter. I'm certain that the prose written at typewriters forty or fifty years ago is different from the prose composed today by writers working at computers. I'm not making a value judgment, I'm just saying they're different. But we're so close to it now we can't see it. This scares me. Some people become impatient with you if you don't sign on to the latest technology. I'm wary of that emotion, this impetuous anger in some people, because all around me I see the disintegration of narrative into piles of "information," and "exposure" to this data passing for learnedness.

TYDEMAN: *Information that never becomes knowledge rarely translates to wisdom.*

LOPEZ: Yes. I have to tell you that in saving so much written material from my life—drafts of stories, correspondence, field notebooks— there have been moments when I thought it was a ridiculous conceit; but other than those fleeting moments of doubt, I've not looked at it that way. What I've thought is this: I was a kid in suburban California whose father abandoned him at the age of five. In the five years after that I was raped repeatedly by another man. Then my family moved to Manhattan—out of a semi-rural existence in California to the fringes of upper-class life in New York. Later, I went to Wyoming and wrangled horses. When it came my time to choose where to live, I moved to Oregon, a landscape I felt comfortable in, and that's been where my life's been anchored ever since. But I'm also somebody who experienced in that time the onset of drug dependency in American culture—prescription drugs, illegal drugs, recreational drugs, enhancement drugs, performance drugs. Prior to 1950, drugs came into play for only a small portion of the culture. After 1950, you see this quantum leap in the consumption of drugs, such that today, people . . . I have no idea what percentage of the population is on prescription drugs—antidepressants, for example; but I, too, have experienced this, been exposed to it. What I have been through—abandonment, abuse, despair, the yearning for "self-actualization"—is the experience of nearly half the people in my generation. If I keep a relatively complete record of what I've experienced, then somebody with a gift for putting things like this together can use the raw material of my life to say, "Here's what happened to one writer during a period of accelerated dehumanizing at the end of the twentieth century and the beginning of the twenty-first." I'm one of those writers working in an area—American postcolonial writing, nature writing, spiritual writing, landscape literature, you choose—that a lot of literary critics don't recognize as a legitimate part of American literature. I'm trying to explore an area between culture and nature that seems to be emerging as an important arena for political writing in American literature. I want to contribute to that, to what's going on around me, create a responsible and responsive body of short stories and essays and books, but I also want to contribute by keeping track of what's been going on around me. It would be my hope that what of mine is in the Sowell Collection here at Texas Tech would end up being about something other than me.

TYDEMAN: *Something that has stuck with me—Harry Stack Sullivan said something along the lines that, as a person, we are like all others, like some others and like no one else. And in a sense, that hierarchy is what you're speaking to . . .*
LOPEZ: Yes.

TYDEMAN: . . . *about the larger cultural dimensions . . .*
LOPEZ: Right.

TYDEMAN: . . . *the times that a writer lives in and the issues that are really forced on him by the culture.*
LOPEZ: Right. When I go back in my journals, which is rarely, one comforting thing I find is that I was struggling with the same ideas at thirty-three, at forty-three and at fifty-three. I come back repeatedly to the same questions, about spiritual need, about justice, the desacralization of the world. I also regain a sense of meaning from knowing that although I wouldn't write the same book all over again, the work taken *together* over four decades makes consistent sense. This book that's coming out in a couple of months, *Resistance*, will strike some people as very political, but, as I think I said to you in a letter, its adumbration is there in a short story called "Light Action in the Caribbean." That particular story is so brutal, some readers fail to see that what's happening to them emotionally at the end is a limning, if you will, of what's happening to us emotionally as a culture. We mock certain shallow elements in our culture, but when these people are harmed and we suddenly feel remorse, we don't see our complicity in their destruction. We don't see that we're *all* food for a monster. No one is exempt from what's coming. And, at the end of that story, the character who should draw our deepest sympathy is . . . I guess some readers miss the last three paragraphs, they're so stunned by what happens to the main characters. Some reviewers blame me, as the writer, for the emotions they're feeling over what happens to these three characters. They shouldn't be blaming me, they should be looking at that hundred-and-eighty-degree reversal in their emotional response to this couple, and wonder what is it about our society that creates these reversals of compassion, and what our complicity in it is, and do they or do they not see how imperiled this poor fisherman is at the end, who's not yet stepped completely *into* this world of turbo-charged American capitalism. So *Resistance* is a book that for some, might . . . I mean, part of what you experience as a writer is that if all anybody knows about you is that you wrote, in my case, *Arctic Dreams*, they'll look at a book like *Resistance* and say, "Well, where did this come from?" It came out of

the same thirty-five years of work. People who have read only my non-fiction sometimes assume that I'm an activist involved in or supporting the event or the phenomenon I'm writing about. People come up to me and ask me to sign onto a campaign that promotes recovery of the wolf, say, without wondering whether I might want to look it over first, or see if what they're doing is relevant to what I'm doing. They confuse their *interpretation* of the book with my intention in writing the book. They believe their interpretation and my intention are the same, which, of course, is the main problem writers have with critics who assume a motive exists in writing something, where none does.

Tydeman: *You said something in your afterword to the new anniversary edition of Of Wolves and Men that I think has some bearing on what we're talking about—the position of the writer in the larger culture and understanding life itself. You wrote that "reality is a mystery . . . and bound to remain so. And it may be as good an idea to live within the mystery as to stand outside, possessed of the notion that it can be explained."*
Lopez: Yes.

Tydeman: *And in your work you point to that fact. You point to the mystery of reality. This seems to be present in your thinking and your work right from the beginning.*
Lopez: Yes. While you were quoting that sentence, I was thinking that I've been saying this for a long time, that living within the mystery is not *better* than attempting to solve the mystery, but it's a way of life as good. In *Of Wolves and Men* I'm trying to suggest that the results of scientific research can't substitute entirely for traditional, indigenous knowledge of a landscape. We need both. Some people have suggested I'm not respectful enough of science. No careful reader, I think, would ever say that. What I will not do is promote a hierarchy where one group of people claims to possess the truth and tells others they must become believers or else, whether it's in religion or some hierarchy of human epistemologies or a brand of fundamentalism in politics. I don't see that life is in any way diminished by immersing yourself in the insolubility of its mysteries. And maybe this is one more element in my trying to make a decision

when I was a freshman at Notre Dame. My major was going to be aeronautical engineering, but in beginning to practice that, I found myself too far on one side of the divide, too far from the humanities. I need that other side. Where I really live is between the two. If you were to read an article about my road-testing a car, in an automotive magazine in 1968, and then read in "Flight" of my fascination with this 747-400 aircraft, you'd see the same imagination at work. Part of what "Flight" is about, to me, is how we took this absolutely amazing machine and did something so short-sighted, banal, and excessive with it. We're a culture that will take a simple drug and jack up its effects until it starts killing people. Cocaine becomes crack cocaine, then you have to do crack cocaine and heroin together. We just keep pushing the rush until it causes a breakdown somewhere—death, boredom, obsolescence. We make these wonderful aircraft, and then it becomes a question of having to have more of them. Everybody has to be able to get anywhere right away now, for whatever reason they have or don't have. Look at cell phones. I sat next to a woman yesterday on a plane who made three or four phone calls *after* the airplane door closed, until she was directly ordered to stop making calls. As soon as we touched down she started calling again. These "conversations" were antic monologues, about whether or not she should return the bikini she just bought, whether another of her girl-friends might want it. This is a desperate attempt, I think, to make connections with people. New technologies aren't going to make this longing for contact go away, they're going to make it worse. Why aren't we ferociously questioning the environment that produces this behavior? What do we tell this woman? More Xanax? Somebody told me they'd seen a survey that showed that in the year 2003 more conversation took place around the world on cell phones than had taken place between human beings since the dawn of human time. How you get a statistic like that, I don't know, but you hear these statements everywhere, our frantic attempt to communicate, to be heard, to be known. A good idea, I suppose, the cell phone, but in this country its potential good is swamped and ultimately destroyed by a neurosis that goes deep. We can't be rid of the feeling, many of us, that we're disappearing.

TYDEMAN: *That makes me think of issues concerning a stillness and silence, your way of being in the field—your field methods. How do we create the proper attitude of attention? You might also say something about your library research methods when you're working on a book like* Arctic Dreams. *At the risk of changing the tone here, I think illuminating some of that might be worthwhile.*

LOPEZ: Being "in the field" is a matter of both good planning and serendipity. It's rare that I go out entirely on my own, with no agreement to tie up with other people. This is partly because I can't requisition a ship or a plane or something and actually get to the situations that I want to be in; so I end up going with people who will be my guides and tutors. I try to choose these people carefully, not just for what they know but because I want to keep reasonable control of the risk factor when I'm going into situations that are dangerous. My preparation for going into the field is usually to read about the landscape I'm headed for, to read what other people's responses have been, both local people and people who were just passing through. There is a general pattern to what I do—reading about a place, contacting people I respect and trust, then jumping in. Most often I take an active role in the work. The last time I went out is a while ago now—four, five years ago—into the interior of Antarctica, to search for meteorites. John Schutt, who led the expedition, is a longtime friend. There were six of us. I probably had more than one-sixth of the responsibility on this trip, because I had a lot of Antarctic experience and three of the other people were brand new to it. John and I and one other man were the senior people. Because of my age and experience I wasn't, anymore, what I had been on these former trips, the least informed member of the group. But I had no special exemption. I still had to hold up my end, do my part of the work everyone else was doing. On something like this, forty-five days in a deep-remote tent camp two hundred miles from the South Pole, there's no place for a supernumerary. I'm usually fully involved in such an expedition from the moment I get up until the moment I go to bed. My hours, typically, are a little bit longer than other people's because at the end of the day I have to take notes that I couldn't take during the day. I remember a time when I was aboard a ship, the *Nathaniel B. Palmer*, on its initial voyage into the Weddell Sea.

I got kidded by some of the scientists on board who told me they were bored out of their minds on the long transit from Louisiana to Antarctica. The joke was that there was no place in this 308-foot ship a human being could crawl into that I hadn't been. I had a set of the ship's blueprints in my room, and my daily explorations of the ship, my inquiries about its equipment, never—to these scientists—seemed to end. I took the same approach to the 747-400 when I was researching "Flight." I wanted to get into every corner. And, you know, there *was* always something to do on the *Palmer* on that long voyage. All my life I'd wanted to learn how to weld, and there was somebody there who let me weld for a while, so I was doing that some days. I developed a good relationship with the captain, and the captain gave me lessons in navigation. Every day for sixty-eight days I was actively involved in something, and I trusted something good would come of it. You know, if you look at a period of research and then look at the article that came out of it, you might be able to determine that on forty-nine of the sixty-eight days nothing occurred that later turned up, explicitly, in the article, but that's not the point. The point is immersion and momentum and dedication; immersion, momentum, and dedication; immersion, momentum, and dedication. That's my method when I'm in the field. What slows me down now is that I can't take the physical punishment I used to be able to, so I'm wary of situations now that would put me under extreme physical or emotional pressure.

This way of working probably first took formal shape in March of 1976, when I went to Alaska to work on *Of Wolves and Men*. The precursors to that trip included going to northern Minnesota in December of 1975 to observe Dave Mech's fieldwork on wolves. But I think the real beginning of my field research pattern was that March '76 trip to Alaska. So it's reading, selecting gear, contacting people, pulling my notebooks together, getting a general idea of what I'm up to, then going and doing that—whatever I called it—immersion, momentum, and dedication.

TYDEMAN: *Dedication? Staying with it every day?*
LOPEZ: Yes. Yes. And sometimes just saying to yourself, too bad if you're dead tired, you've got to work on your notes. When I'm out

there I'm taking a lot of notes about things that I don't understand. I'm getting some things explained to me, and I know I can contact those people again and go over it again, because I probably won't get all of it the first time. I won't get all of it right. When I come home, that's when the second phase of the library work begins. In interviews with my companions I'll have learned about a lot of obscure articles or books, publications I don't know about—haven't come upon—that succinctly describe a particular part of the event I've become interested in, but that I didn't know about before I went. Having experienced it, I can then go and get those publications out of a library. So, the library work that precedes a trip is not as extensive, or as pointed, as it is when I get back. And then after I make an outline for the piece, there may be an additional little bit of library work, because I see I'm going to be writing about this event instead of the other one. Also, a book I thought I wouldn't get to I'll now check out, because I see it's going to be part of the story.

An important thing to take away from all of this is that I am a student of the knowledge the people I'm traveling with possess. Some of these people might have written some of it down and I can go find that. Other people don't write. They never wrote anything down. They just know, and from the beginning with them you try to listen closely. This nonfiction methodology, for me, is a process of apprenticeship, of being tutored.

An interesting psychological thing for me, now, is that when I first started doing this kind of thing, I tended to be among the younger people in the group. Now I'm often the oldest. I've been in the field with some individuals whose impulse was to treat me like an undergraduate. I didn't appreciate it. You experience these emotions in any situation in which a professor treats you as though you had no meaning outside his instruction. That's another reason I choose the people I go into the field with very carefully. But sometimes I'm in a situation where the only person who has the expertise I want is somebody I don't really get along with. You just go, and make the best of it.

If you told me today I could walk out the door and do whatever I wanted, it would be this kind of fieldwork. I have a very active life with public speaking and working with other individuals who are as scared as I am about the political situation in the country today. I have obligations in several arenas; but if I were utterly free to do what I wanted to do, I'd pack a bag and walk out the door for Western China or any of half a dozen other places—Australia, the interior of Venezuela—and immerse myself. Some of the happiest times of my life have come during those moments of apprenticeship in remote areas, traveling with people I hardly knew but who knew a lot about where we were. There's something, I guess, from my childhood about that. My childhood reveals an inordinate enthusiasm for getting outdoors.

TYDEMAN: *Getting on your bike and . . .*

LOPEZ: Getting on my bike and riding away. Some of those scenes in "A Scary Abundance of Water." In some of my short fiction there's a pattern, a younger man trying to experience a world in which some sort of expert resides. And here's a way, I guess, in which the fiction and the nonfiction are connected. The young narrator in "Teal Creek" who seeks out the advice of, or is affected by the training of, the anchorite in the story is fascinated by that man. That relationship—he sneaks up on his remote cabin and spies on him—that psychological set-up, the outsider, fascinated by the expertise of someone peripheral to society, that's a foundation block in my fiction. In my nonfiction, a similar thing is being acted out, and then reflected on. In fiction, the way the story usually works, whatever's going to happen after the narrator experiences these emotions, happens "off the page," after the short story is over. What happens in nonfiction is that *I* go through a similar emotional encounter after the research ends. What happens after is that I write an essay.

TYDEMAN: *One of the students of your writing has suggested the importance of the quest, or the quest narrative in your work . . .*
LOPEZ: Right.

TYDEMAN: *. . . and that sounds to me similar to what you're talking about.*
LOPEZ: You know, what we're talking about I've never thought about much before, which is one reason I like talking to you. I don't feel

I need to protect myself. I want to push into this, then, and try to make some sense out of it. And finding these things . . . realizing that if here's fifty books on the table and the one I'll pick up is about the Percival legend or *Moby-Dick* or *Don Quixote*. I guess these questing, episodic encounters with the world are what I want to be about. My life *is* a kind of questing. As I said, if I could walk out the door, what I'd choose is a quest. I've just been thinking about this, that most of my going-to-sleep dreams take the form of quests. In that half-dream state I'm imagining mounting a horse, or getting in my truck to travel some great distance. I have to think this is where a story like "The Interior of North Dakota" comes from. The narrator or quester there, encountering a part of the North Dakota landscape that's not known because the maps are skewed. When I go to bed at night, I think about taking off the same way the main character does in "The Construction of the *Rachel*." He just takes off, drives across Nevada, and ends up at that monastery. That's how many of my going-to-sleep dreams start. And horses, you know. . . . Well, horses figure in a large part of what I imagine, the impressions that carry over from those two summers I spent wrangling horses in Wyoming. It's part of the foundation for *Crow and Weasel*, it's in "Stolen Horses." These narratives are the reifications of what I imagined when I was nineteen or twenty, working on that dude ranch. In the evenings, I also worked on an inept translation of the *Aeneid*. In my senior year in prep school we translated part of the *Aeneid*, and I remained fascinated with the process. I remember many evenings sitting there in my cabin, the sawdust stove going, my room-mate, Lance, studying for veterinary school, and me at my little table, translating the *Aeneid* with my Latin grammar and dictionaries. And then, four-thirty in the morning, we'd be up and out the door, waling up our wrangle horses. When I was moving horses up from the Snake River into the corrals in the morning, what was going through my head once in a while was how to translate some complicated phrase I'd quit on the night before. Lance was the only person who knew what I was doing. It was business that stayed in our cabin.

TYDEMAN: *This may be a stretch, so correct me.*
LOPEZ: Well, we're doing okay for stretches. I mean these kinds of

things—what was I thinking, trying to translate that book?—they're fascinating for me to consider. I was trying to live the life I'd later invent for characters in my stories.

TYDEMAN: *That combination you just described, the physical labor, the hard work, carrying the water, chopping the wood, combined with the intellectual side, the translation—isn't that close to the monastic ideal?*
LOPEZ: Oh yes. You know, in November of 1966 I went to Gethsemani, Thomas Merton's monastery in Kentucky, to see if that was the place for me. One vivid image I retain is watching two men, in some sort of conversation of easy gestures, walking together toward a dairy barn. I thought, "This is my whole thing: physical labor and a spiritual life." Another image I retain is going to the chapel at dawn and seeing all these work boots and coveralls neatly hung up and aligned outside. These were the habiliments of devout, working people. Inside were these men in their stocking feet and monastic robes, preparing, as Joseph Campbell said once, to witness "the greatest act of white magic in the history of Western culture." That combination of things was everything I wanted out of life. Or so I thought. I made a decision the next day to leave. Whatever my work was supposed to be, this was too perfect, and at too young an age. Somewhere else was where I needed to go.

I remember standing next to my car before I departed, looking at the monastery, the way it's laid out, and thinking that whatever I was going to do would look like this, but it would be more invisible, not so institutionalized. From there I went to St. Louis, where Sandy was in school. Seven months later we would get married. I remember her saying to me once, "How could you have still been considering such a monumental change in your life when we were engaged to be married?" It was a discomforting question. My commitment to the marriage was deep. It was a marriage that lasted almost thirty years. But there was still this unanswered question for me, about the monastic life. When I was a senior at Loyola, a Jesuit prep school in Manhattan, it was a tradition that toward the end of the school year the seniors would travel to a seminary and spend three days there on retreat. The idea was to take some major question in your life and devote your energy to its elucidation, its clarification. The question for me was, Should I go to a university or should I enter the seminary? At the end of three days I had a clear sense the answer was no, not the seminary. When I graduated from Notre Dame, the same question came back. I thought, I've got to get this straightened out. So I went to Gethsemane. Leaning toward a monastic life, though, that's in a lot of the fiction I've written. And there's another accident here, you know. My biological father was Roman Catholic, and, because he was, he refused to divorce his first wife. He just abandoned her and their son and married my mother, so he was a bigamist. My mother never converted to Catholicism, but she insisted, after my father abandoned us, that my brother and I be baptized and raised Roman Catholic. Later she married a nominal Roman Catholic, my twice-divorced stepfather. How I ended up a once-devout Roman Catholic is a long story. My mother was a teacher—she taught junior high and junior college—and at that time the Catholic schools in the San Fernando Valley were superior to the public schools. Mother believed in the best education, so that was part of it. I was baptized when I was five and went to Catholic school from first grade on. The Jesuit approach to spirituality became my own take on Roman Catholicism, so that left a lot of latitude for metaphorical maneuvering within the theology and iconography of Roman Catholicism.

TYDEMAN: *Your introduction to the Desert Fathers and the monastic tradition, did that come before college?*
LOPEZ: Oh, yes. Sure. It ran all through the six years I was at Loyola, from the seventh to twelfth grades. Yes, that's where that came from. Maybe not actually reading the Desert Fathers, but the preparation for reading them was there. I've gone back to this question about quest, and I find the elements of quest and the elements of Roman Catholicism intertwined, which is why the Percival legend reverberates so strongly for me. I'd have to say, though, that I don't see my life as any kind of quest for the Grail. The Grail is often understood as the cup from the Last Supper. What the cup stands for, in my imagination, is the sharing of food, the nurturing of community. If I do have a Grail quest, it's to understand how to induce that, how to diminish the cult

of the individual and increase the authority of the community, how to underscore the need to share.

TYDEMAN: *How can I be of service? Another area, Barry, that I think hasn't been talked about enough or understood completely, is your collaborative work with other artists. This begins in your undergraduate years.*
LOPEZ: Yes, with Justin Soleta.

TYDEMAN: *At Notre Dame. Could you talk some about that?*
LOPEZ: One guess about where this impulse to collaborate comes from is knowing that, early on, I was trying to express myself in two different ways, as a writer and as a photographer. I wasn't interested in collaborating as a photographer with other writers, but I did like trying to respond as a writer to other photographers. Justin Soleta was an older fellow working at *Ave Maria* magazine, where some of my first stories were published—by Jim Andrews, who later went on to found Andrews McMeel. Justin would photograph migrant workers, for example, or make a series of photographs of a carved crucifix illuminated in different ways, and I'd write a text in response. We collaborated on three or four pieces for *Ave Maria*. At that time, as a senior at Notre Dame, I was also acting in theater productions at St. Mary's College, where I was taking theater courses, and I'd been working in radio since I was a freshman. I had a working awareness, in other words, of trying to communicate ideas and emotions—over the radio, on stage, as a photographer, and as a writer—but little expertise, of course. I liked the ensemble feeling of theater and radio, and that appreciation for working with other people has come and gone, I guess, through my life. I've always liked the *idea* of working with somebody else, but I'm not always pursuing it. Part of what I like about collaboration is the chance to discover something that neither person would have, working alone. That's what theater is like when it's all clicking one night, something extra-worldly happens, like what happens with a rock-and-roll band or a jazz group when the music gets seamless, when it starts to run. "You just hope you have the brains to get out of the way," is what they say. I like that feeling. My sense is that, if we, as a culture, don't get back to a very strong awareness of community, if we continue to

support the eminence of individuals, it's going to bring us to trouble.

I've had a number of artist, writer, and photographer friends along the way. They've continued their work, and we stay in regular touch. So, a community of artists and writers has always been part of my reference system. Even after I stopped photographing in 1981 I stayed in close touch with photographers. I was working with magazines, so of course I sometimes had the opportunity to work with a photographer I knew. There was a certain measure of selfishness in this, on occasion. Sometimes, I know, I wanted to drive the whole thing. With *Crow and Weasel*, it was Tom Pohrt's idea that we do a book together, but that that book would be *Crow and Weasel* was my suggestion, and there were times I probably crowded Tom's creative impulses. We built a deep friendship, and a wonderful book came out of it, but Tom deferred to me on issues where he might have wanted to go another way. He gave me a gift. I never forget that.

I've just finished *Resistance*, a work of fiction that includes nine monotypes by Alan Magee, and we hit a few rough spots around that. He and I talked many times about our mutual discomfort—anger, really—with Republican administrations at the close of the twentieth century—especially what the two Bush administrations were doing in the Middle East. We seethed around these issues, and talked about them from the point of view of an artist and a writer. What to do? We talked about collaborating. I was profoundly struck by this set of faces he had done, these monotypes. I wanted to collaborate with him around those images. I didn't have any clear idea what that might be, I just knew we both felt compelled to do something, to say something. I imagined a fine press limited edition book, a book that then might come out later as a trade book, but that, first would offer Alan high-quality reproduction of his work, and me a venue for whatever I was going to write. In the summer of 2002 I sat down and, very quickly, over a period of just a few weeks, I drafted this manuscript I called *Resistance*. Once I drafted the manuscript, I realized it had a level of complexity, and was of such a length, that I needed to talk to Knopf, my publisher, about it. Then I went through probably the longest rewriting process of any major project I've ever worked on. Usually a manuscript goes through about five drafts with me. This went through seven. The reason for that is that it's not actually a collection of stories, nor is it a novel. It's somewhere in between, and it was difficult to solve some of the technical problems.

One thing that happens in collaborations, one way in which collaborations can go wrong, is that when a writer and a photographer begin work on a project in separate spheres or out of phase, each is imagining a different kind of book that might come out of it. It's the publisher, though, in trade publishing, who really determines what that book is going to look like. So, the more I talked with my editor at Knopf, the more I understood this collaboration was headed toward a trade work of fiction. Alan gave it his blessing. He just wanted to be sure his work wasn't perceived as a set of illustrations for *Resistance*. So it's made clear in a statement at the front of the book that Alan created those images before the stories were written, that there was a larger body of work from which I chose these particular images. His work stimulated mine, his images enhance the book, and his allowing them to be so imperfectly reproduced was, again, a gift.

With *Of Wolves and Men* I ran into a major problem with a photographer. He was taking pictures of wolves at the Biosocial Research Center at the University of Oregon and trying to get Ken Kesey, a mutual friend, to write a book with him. And it turned out, Ken decided not to do that. This fellow introduced himself to me, or somebody introduced the two of us and said, "Well, you two guys should collaborate." He was a nice enough fellow, I liked his photographs, and we had a good relationship. We used some of his photographs in the initial nonfiction pieces I wrote. Then I saw what I really wanted to do with a book about these animals. The photographer remained more interested in a book that would be a vehicle for his photographs. As it turned out, the book designer, in consultation with the publisher, created a book in which that photographer's work didn't play a very large role. Collaboration is never smooth. It requires a certain amount of deference on both parts, and where you run into trouble with it, either me with somebody else or somebody else with me, is with the egos that produce the work one or the other of you is attracted to. When you enter into a loose and informal agreement to do something together, you most often do so out of enthusiasm for each other's work. And then there can be a bit of a struggle.

I've written catalog essays for Richard Rowland, a potter; for Rick Bartow, a mixed-media artist/painter/carver; and for another maskmaker, ceramicist, and mixed-media artist named Lillian Pitt. In each instance I've had a body of work to respond to. I've also written a brief catalog essay for a show of Alan's. But I wouldn't call those collaborations. They're my expression of homage to people whose work I admire, work I want to take some role in promoting. In those instances, how the catalog is designed or what else might be in it, that's none of my business and I don't get involved. Alan and I recorded and edited a long interview we did with each other, about what it means to be an artist or a writer in modern society, and it was published in Alan's new book, *Alan Magee: Paintings, Sculpture, Graphics.* The book is Alan's book, and what he chose to put in that book was his own business. As far as the involvement of my own ego goes, all I wanted was to be able to edit my part of the interview.

I wonder, you know, whether you can maintain your vision if you let yourself go in somebody else's work. Being in the theater is not like being a writer. Playing in an orchestra is not like being a photographer. Collaboration is hard. I like to associate with people whose work I admire, to see if there's a way to do that, and I enjoy promoting the work of other people; but I do come out of some collaborative experiences thinking, "Next time, I'll just do it on my own."

TYDEMAN: (laughter) *Easier just to do it on my own.*
LOPEZ: Yes.

TYDEMAN: *To extend the example further, the dramatization, making into a play,* Crow and Weasel.
LOPEZ: Bob Redford bought the stage rights to the play and hired a playwright, Jim Leonard, Jr. He brought Jim and me together at Sundance and, let's see, I think almost right away Redford's production people were contacted by the Children's Theatre in Minneapolis. Some executives at Target, the retailer, which is headquartered in Minneapolis, had read the book and loved it and they wanted the Children's Theatre to produce a play. Redford's people knew the Children's Theatre

was the best venue for children's theater in the country, so they were happy to let them co-produce. The director, Gary Gisselman, came in from Minneapolis to Redford's place in Utah, and Jim Leonard, myself, and the director, all started work on the play. There was quite a bit of tension between Jim Leonard and me. I think Jim just didn't want me working in an area—playwriting and stagecraft—where he had expertise, and I respected that about him. I tried to make clear to him that I was not looking for a way to move my name up on the playbill, but trying to make sure that this deceptively simple book wasn't inadvertently compromised by somebody who did not have a background with Native American culture. So Jim and I had our difficult moments. I think Jim sometimes felt that I was treating him like hired help, and there were times I felt like Jim was treating me like an anthropologist instead of a writer. But we came to respect each other's expertise. Jim came to me at one point and said that he was delighted by what we'd discovered together, and that he appreciated my willingness to work in a theatrical medium instead of a writer's medium. I had suggested a way to solve a scene that afternoon and he had turned to me and said, "Now, *that's* theater." It wasn't a suggestion about language, it was about movement. He came to me that night and said that absolutely the right thing to do was for us to share the credit for writing the play. I was profoundly moved, but, as it turned out, we decided to go another way with the credits. Gary Gisselman did the most to smooth out the tension between Jim and me. He had Jim Leonard's respect as a director, and my respect as well.

When I came to Redford's people at the start of all this, I said, "I know this is going to sound bad because this person is a close friend of mine, but the best composer we could get here would be John Luther Adams." I said, "I brought a tape of his music. I'm going to ask you to contact him and at least give him the opportunity to make a presentation." Redford's producer came to me after he listened to the tape and said, "Well, the only question I've got is when can we get this guy here?" I'd worked with John Adams on a number of projects before this. John was a close friend of the poet John Haines, and Haines had written a series of poems called *Forest without Leaves*, based on his experiences around Sudbury, Ontario, around the nickel mines, seeing all of these trees standing dead in the spring. Leafless trees. His poems evoke the sense of an industrial wasteland. John scored *Forest without Leaves* for orchestra and voice and asked me to come to the opening in Fairbanks and make a presentation, in which I talked about collaborative work—his with John Haines, mine with John Adams, et cetera. So I did. Another good friend, Dick Nelson, received a grant from ARCO to do a five-part series based on his book *Make Prayers to the Raven*. Dick asked me to do the voice-over for that show and John Adams to do the music for it. So, that was another way John and I were brought together to collaborate. But when Redford said, "We want this guy to do the music for *Crow and Weasel*," suddenly we were talking about a major collaborative effort, with a lot of ego tension. It would call for a lot of give and take, a lot of deference and adjustment.

One of the things Gisselman did in the second year we all worked at Sundance was to talk with the actors, most of whom were urban people, about how physically to be in the woods. He said to me one day, "I want you to give me twenty-five things an actor could do walking across the tundra that don't require any language, but which the actors can use to develop a sense of being fully involved in the theatrical space." When the play was in production in Minneapolis, I took the actors out to a Nature Conservancy preserve and worked with them. If you saw a deer two hundred yards away over there, I said, here's how two starving men would approach that deer, how they would use various signs to communicate with each other. When we came across animal tracks, I showed them how you could tell by the moisture still in the paw print and the degree of its collapse how old it might be. I got them to look at different kinds of vegetation, to see what animals were feeding on, and we looked for the husks of nuts and seeds and things like that. I think a smart thing Gisselman did here was give me some sort of credibility in the actors' eyes that didn't trespass, in any way, on Jim Leonard's expertise as the playwright. So the actors were saying, "Well, I'm getting this stuff from Barry, I'm getting this other stuff from Jim, and the guy running it all is Gary." I'll never forget Gary's tact and poise, his generosity. He asked me the first time we met to give him a list of twenty books he should read in order to get some grounding in a Native American way of seeing the land. I thought to myself, "This guy will never read twenty books. I'll give him a list of twenty, he may read three or four, and that would be great." He read all twenty. And the next year when we got back together at Sundance he asked me for a list of another twenty. So this guy . . . I mean, there are a few times in your life when you know that if it weren't for this one person. . . .

TYDEMAN: *He was the catalyst.*

LOPEZ: He also got on to something in my own work that I've never talked about, but that I want to write an essay about one day. That was more than ten years ago, but you just don't forget the guidance in a collaboration like that. You know, when we were doing *Crow and Weasel,* I had been close with John Adams for a long time. He contacted me once and said, "I've been reading these Trickster stories of yours.* I want to think about a theatrical production." He'd been talking to his friend, Molly Smith, the director at Perseverance Theater in Douglas, Alaska. Perseverance had funding from the state to do one production a year based on Native American material. Perseverance had done what became a very famous Eskimo production of *Antigone.* They did a lot of great things in that run of shows. So, Molly Smith and John decided to do this play called *Coyote,* in 1987. I adapted the book, John worked on the music, and then John and I and Molly and a choreographer all got together at the theater with the musicians and actors. John and I loved working together. It's not like Jim Leonard and me trying to work together, two writers, or me trying to work with Tom Pohrt or Alan Magee, where there's just the two of us, you know. When John and I work together, there's more of an ensemble thing going on. It involves musicians and actors. Molly, John, and I working together on this production with a choreographer meant we had four different egos. There were too many people for you to remain at loggerheads with any one person. Somebody else was always breaking up the tension. Molly later became the artistic director at Arena Stage in Washington, D.C., and two years ago we produced *Coyote* there. I didn't do very much with the Washington production. I came once,

---

Giving Birth to Thunder.

saw the actors, talked to them a little bit, but I really didn't do much. The music had already been written, and Molly knew she could just take it from there.

TYDEMAN: *Didn't you also write for one of the Adams's compositions, a short story? What is that?*

LOPEZ: No, that was with David Darling and Manfred Eicher. Manfred runs ECM in Munich. He's the person who helped put Arvo Pärt* on the world map. He's been Keith Jarrett's producer for years, he produced Pat Metheny and all these people, Jan Garbarek, Gavin Bryars, the Hilliard Ensemble, a long list. He told me he was looking for some different kind of liner note. I told him I'd been thinking about that too, and asked him if he would give me a CD of music with no language. "Maybe just one composer and a single instrument," I said. Then I'd try to write a story in emotional parallel to it. "All I need," I told him, "is the music played in the order it'll be on the CD, and no instruction—no annotations, no titles for individual pieces. Just the music." So he selected a cellist named David Darling, not knowing that David and I knew each other. I got the music and wrote a story, and it appeared in the liner notes the way I had asked—just my title, the story, my name, and a copyright symbol. No instructions about whether you were supposed to read the story while listening to the music, or read it later, or first, or try to pace it to the music. The idea was: here's language, here's the music. If you don't want to put them together, don't. If you want to throw the story away, fine. So, yes, that was another kind of collaboration.

A producer named Mickey Houlihan, who had worked for some years with the Paul Winter Consort, introduced me to David Darling. We were all together on a river trip Paul arranged in 1980 or 1981 through the Grand Canyon, about which I wrote a piece.**

TYDEMAN: *Yes, I remember.*

---

*Arvo Pärt (1935–), internationally renowned Estonian composer of modern classical music and sacred works, now residing in Berlin and Tallinn.
**"Gone Back into the Earth" (1981).

LOPEZ: It was on that trip that Mickey said, "I want to get you and David Darling in a studio." I said I'd enjoy that, too, but what prompted the idea? He said, "It's just an intuition. Something good will come out of it." We all went home, and I got this phone call later from Mickey saying, "Look, I know this is kind of off the wall, but if you want to step into it I'll pick up the expense." So David and I went to Boulder—actually to Mickey's place in Erie, Colorado—and recorded. Mickey wanted to work with the language in *River Notes*, my voice, and David's cello. Neither David nor I knew what to expect, but I taught myself something in that recording session. It got really interesting when I was silent. There were places in the recording where I just stopped speaking and left the acoustic space open for David to fill with these big major chords. The emotional thrill of allowing music to be something other than background on a spoken recording was something that all three of us got excited about. I remember Mickey bringing us into the studio and showing us how the tones of David's cello music and the tones of my voice overlapped in a certain way, that that was what he had intuited on the river. Looking back, probably what convinced me that future collaborations were a possibility for me was how the music, the voice, and the story together became such a different thing from the book, that it was okay to bring somebody else into your territory and let them invent. David and I saw each other only a couple of times after that. It was the same year Jim Andrews* died, because we dedicated the album to him. When we finished *River Notes*, we were so full of energy, so full of enthusiasm for each others' work, we thought, you know, if Mickey can pay the bills, the hotel, the airfare, the meals, why not go to work on *Desert Notes*? We tried. A total failure. Disaster. None of us liked it. We were over the top from the start. We couldn't modulate it. None of us understood how to make it lean. That book has a very different energy from *River Notes*. We've talked for years about getting together again, but we never have. Two or three years ago, at Sun Valley in Idaho, David and I were asked to work together again

---

*Jim Andrews of Andrews McMeel had published the book the year before.

in front of an audience, to improvise. I read a piece David had never seen and he played his cello up against the story as it unfolded. We fell into the rhythm we'd had twenty-two years before, where I would just finish a phrase and disappear and the music would fill the room until there was some invitation for me to come back in. David and I looked at each other with raised eyebrows after that performance. The audience shot to its feet. It was, again, one of those things where you say to yourself as a performer, "Where did *that* come from?" You don't know where it comes from. David said "Absolutely *unbelievable*, not to see each other for years and then create something bigger than either one of us could have made." And the response of that audience, which didn't know what to expect. Some standing ovations—in some ways the most beautiful—grow slowly, as people realize what's happened, and then the whole house is standing. The other standing ovation is that one where, while the last tone is still alive, everybody *leaps* to their feet. Everybody, including the performers, knows they've been in the presence of something magical.

So, these collaborative experiences have mostly been with people I love. In the collaboration with David and Mickey, I saw it was possible for somebody to take my work and make it grow—find another dimension in it—and then I could find another dimension in the language. There's a painter in Australia, John Wolseley—well, I may have let this one go too long. I met John in 1989 and ever since have wanted to go into the bush with him. He's a well-known landscape painter. His work is in major collections and museums in Australia, but he's very open and unassuming. I love the way he *thinks* about landscape, and I've wanted to go on a trip with him and try to write about how he paints. It would be a story in some way akin to "Effleurage," where I was so taken with the integrity and imagination of Richard Rowland, the same thing would drive this piece. I've wanted to do that with other people, find language that paid homage to their work. That's why I agreed to speak at the opening of Bob Adams's* show at the

---

*Robert Adams (1937–), American photographer, known for his landscape studies of the American West. His exhibition *True West* was held in 2001 at the Amon Carter Museum of American Art in Fort Worth, Texas.

Amon Carter, where it came as such a surprise to the curator that we didn't know each other. We just respected each other's work.

TYDEMAN: *Would you describe your work with Robin Eschner as collaboration? Or is it something else?*

LOPEZ: No, not exactly collaboration. Cooperation. "Apologia" already existed as an essay. She called me and said, "I want to respond to this, if that's all right with you," and, knowing her work, I said, "Oh, my goodness, yes, of course." The book then, *Apologia*, is really Robin's vision and invention—a great thing, I believe, to come out of that "collaboration."

What I think of as true collaboration is Gary Gisselman getting Jim Leonard, me, and John Adams to put our stuff together to make that play come to life. Cooperation is a lesser form of collaboration. You cooperate with someone whose vision you trust. That's where most limited edition fine print books come from, and that work with Robin is a good example. Another time she came to me and said, "I've been reading your work for a long while and I want to do a series of paintings in response to it. Would you let me take some paragraphs from books and use them like legends, next to the paintings?" I was flattered, of course, and now she's done that twice.

Apololgia involved seven people, with Chuck Hobson as the designer. Well, the book was sort of already designed before Chuck agreed to work with us, because of the way Robin envisioned this accordion-fold, twenty-three-panel wood block image. But Chuck got all these people together—the binder, the edition printer, the letterpress printer. We selected Sandy Tilcock at lone goose press as the publisher. I'd worked with her before and knew she could also design and assemble the clamshell boxes for the book. She also worked with me to print those tire-print maps that went with the book. I told Chuck at that time, "I want you to know I have great respect for your work, and I know a lot of pieces were already in place when you came in on this project. I'd like to do something else with you where you can start the design from scratch." So that's where *Anotaciones* came from. Now he's working on a fine print edition of "The Mappist."

I love working with good friends whose work, you know, I would admire even if I didn't know them. Frans Lanting, the photographer, and I have tried a couple of times to get together on projects. We've done some calendars and did an article once about snow geese. Maybe someday he and I will do something else. Bob Adams has asked me to do a catalog essay for him, but when the time came I had to say that it wasn't possible, I just didn't have the time then. (I feel like I still owe him on that.) The only time I can remember there being a genuine interest in the film rights to a story of mine was with "Emory Bearhand's Birds," from *Light Action in the Caribbean*. It didn't go anywhere, but that's something I've always wanted to do. You know, it's one of those clichéd, pedestrian desires, but I'd just like to sit in a darkened theater one day and see something that started out in my mind come alive on the screen. Two or three dance companies, in Berkeley and New York, have developed productions and staged them, choreographic interpretations.

I guess, over time, there's been a lot of collaboration, or cooperation.

TYDEMAN: *Yes, there has. I was going to pick up on that earlier thread, because you've mentioned that photography got you thinking about collaboration, but where did your interest in photography begin? Was that in high school? Was it in college?*

LOPEZ: No, it was a trip I took with my brother, Dennis. This would have been June, July, and August of 1964. We got a vehicle from my uncle who had a Dodge dealership in Sedalia, Missouri. He loaned us a pickup with a little camper on the back. Dennis and I drove out to California from New Jersey, and up into British Columbia and Alberta, and then back down into the West. We might have then driven back to Sedalia and flown home, I don't actually remember. But I started taking photographs on that trip. I remember getting myself a real camera, a Pentax 35 mm reflex camera, in the summer of 1965. In 1965 and 1966, when I was a senior at Notre Dame, I was taking a lot of photographs and using some of them to illustrate stories I was writing. I think probably my association with Justin Soleta intensified my desire to work solely in black and white, but I didn't particularly like being in the darkroom, so friends sometimes printed my work, which would always be the case for me with black and white. I concentrated on 35 mm color work, and the move to Oregon in 1968 gave me a landscape to photograph that was very stimulating. Just before I left South Bend I collaborated with a guitarist named Chuck Perrin. He improvised a piece of guitar work around some sixty or seventy of my images, and we produced that slide show in South Bend probably early in the spring of 1968. I haven't seen him since, you know, so that's thirty-six years ago. But the essay I wrote, "Learning to See," picks up right after that, during the early part of my photographic work. I don't remember . . .

TYDEMAN: *An incident or . . .*
LOPEZ: No. Just that in the summer of 1965, just before I went back to work in Wyoming at Triangle X, I bought a camera.

TYDEMAN: *Even after you made the decision to give up photography you maintained a lively interest in photography. You've written about wildlife photography and about the photographers whose work you admire, but you've also raised some important questions about the choice of subject and where authority rests in the photographic process. I think it would be important to have you elucidate some of that.*
LOPEZ: That thinking is the result of my own wondering about what I was doing as a photographer. And conversations, mostly with Frans Lanting and Robert Adams, and a little bit with Galen Rowell, about the manipulation of images. My position was that in the history of wildlife photography, the photograph derived its authority from the authority of the animal. If the animal was doing something and you photographed it, there was no question about whether or not the animal was actually doing that. If there were six hyenas in a photograph, the assumption was there were six hyenas there when you took the photograph. But once things like Photoshop came along, it became possible for people to put twelve hyenas in the photograph if they wanted to, and my objection, and I think the objection of most photographers, to that manipulation is not that it's wrong, or that you don't have a right to do this. What's wrong is marketing or promoting that photograph as authentic, when the authority for the photograph now rests with the *photographer*. The photographer is now the

authority behind the image, not the subject. And that distinction is an important one to keep making. I don't object to anybody making an image. What I object to is somebody making *up* an image and then promoting it—or allowing it to be promoted—as something that actually occurred. And of course, that's the difference I have emphasized between fiction and nonfiction. I have the same visceral objection to a memoir that includes significant pieces that are made up. It's not fair to the reader. You're asking the reader for an emotional response based on the authority of the story when the authority lies with your imagination, not with the life you actually lived. You're making more of yourself, wanting the reader's admiration or pity or something—but you've not earned it. Where is it, I wonder, that I talked about this? Did you and I talk about this in the first interview?

TYDEMAN: *No. We talked about the relationship between photo and text and the difficulty there. But no, we didn't talk about wildlife photography. We had a couple of telephone conversations about it.** *

LOPEZ: I talked to somebody, I think, about this. I'm at the stage of my life now where I can't remember where some of these things are, but . . .

TYDEMAN: *Well, there was also another dimension to this that we talked about which you've also written about and that's the reluctance—the inability—of photo editors at wildlife magazines to accept images of animals that don't coincide with the regal, magnificent, or beautiful.*

LOPEZ: Right. When I was photographing, I used to ask other landscape photographers to consider that the Sierra Club and Audubon calendars they were shooting for were not all that different from the Playboy calendars these photographers would never associate themselves with. They were consciously trying to create gorgeous, overwhelming images. They created them in response to an ideal about the beauty of landscape that was, qualitatively I think, no different

---

*The related topics of where authority and authenticity reside in a photograph do arise in the first interview. The example adduced there happens to be a wildlife photo, of a polar bear. The difference of emphasis may explain the uncertainty here.

from men choosing certain types of bodies and arranging them in certain kinds of poses to mirror a set of expectations that American men associate with erotic feminine beauty. Some people were outraged by the suggestion, but I would make it anyway. My argument was, "You say that you want to see landscapes preserved, but what you're photographing are the voluptuous landscapes, so I'm having trouble believing this if there are no photographs of the beauty inherent in an ordinary landscape." This is one of the ways advertising and public relations have compromised art and writing, you know, in the twentieth century. Advertising has become a force for corruption, in my mind, as far as language and imagery are concerned. Its goal is to please the person who's selling something and to induce someone else to buy the product, and it consistently violates the bounds of good taste and offers fatuous expressions—"pushing the envelope," "freedom of expression"—to defend what it's doing. As time goes by, it's an industry I've come to have little respect for, although I have known people working in advertising whom I still hold in some regard. I've worked in it myself. It's just become so compromised.

TYDEMAN: *To complete the circle, you are concerned about zoos and animals as they are caged and kept confined for presumably educational purposes.*

LOPEZ: John Berger has an essay about zoos—"Why Look at Animals?"—that was a seminal piece for me. One thought at its center is that zoos are the last vestige of colonialism. I was so struck by that, by his own ethical stance. He put into words what had become over the years more and more and more distressing for me about zoos. Like most American kids, I went to zoos when I was young, and I liked being there I guess—I don't remember. But as I grew older, I didn't want to be anywhere near them. The argument that zoos introduce children to wild animals has virtually no credibility for me, because children today are introduced to so many things through special effects, through carefully edited and manipulative television programs, that the living animal standing there in a box doesn't have as much authority as it once did. The reasons most often given for zoos to exist are specious to me. The idea that they function as gene pools is misleading. Very few species in any given ecosystem can survive in captivity and produce animals capable of going back and repopulating an area. Most ethologists subscribe to the idea that an animal learns its behavior by growing up in a certain environment. An animal isn't a car, fine-tuned in a garage somewhere, that you then put out on the street. That's not how animals work. So the two major arguments for the existence of zoos—that they educate and that they're a bulwark against loss of diversity—neither of those seems good to me. If you banned zoos, it would force people who really want these animals to survive to face the fact that we're going to have to leave them be in the places where they live and go to whatever length is required to visit them. And that has to mean limited visitation. I think what would happen, though, if you banned zoos, is that wild animals on their native ground would be forgotten. The strongest argument for zoos is that they're the one place civilization provides where animals can come to sing for their supper. Until we achieve another sort of Enlightenment, they are going to have to do this to survive. I have to ask you to excuse me on this. I'm barely rational when it comes to zoos.

In the world we live in, if you have enough money, we believe you should be able to do whatever you want, travel wherever you wish, you know, which takes us to another topic. What's happened in my generation to travel writers? Now, if you describe a place in an evocative way, you're opening the door to its inundation, thousands of people looking for yet one more new thing to do. I was *stunned*—that's the word—when I heard from some wilderness outfitters in Canada that they had built their businesses around the response to *Arctic Dreams,* that the book had awakened such interest in the Arctic that people started booking it as a destination. And with "The Stone Horse"— that's the first piece I wrote where I was deliberately misleading about directions, about where the place was. I didn't want it found. The horse, the ground glyph there, was too vulnerable to vandalism. Three years ago somebody sent me a photograph of the glyph. He wrote that it didn't look that disturbed to him, but when I opened the envelope and looked at the print I saw immediately that it had been compromised. Dozens of the artist's rocks had been removed. To this guy it still held up as a ground glyph, but from the time I first saw it to that date—seventeen years—it had been all but ruined. So many people who had come to visit felt compelled to take away a souvenir. The lesson is, you can't keep people away from a place. John McPhee once wrote an article for *The New Yorker* about a restaurant. I think it was the only time he declined to share the location of a place he'd written about. He wanted to describe the experience of eating at this restaurant but not have it inundated with people. The owner didn't need more people. They didn't need any advertising. And within, I don't know, a week or two weeks of the story coming out, somebody found the place. And *that* became the news story, that somebody found the place John was trying to protect. A friend said to me, "John should have known that if you're going to write a story for *The New Yorker* about a restaurant in the greater New York area and describe it as the epitome of fine eating and not tell anybody where it is, there are going to be *thousands* of people searching for that restaurant, and somebody's going to find it. It's just too attractive a prize to be ignored."

I'm still thinking about something we spoke about earlier, about how much my life is changing, working with Texas Tech, making these public presentations around the country, working on *Home Ground.* *Some days I would trade the whole thing just to be able to go out the door and climb on a plane with my gear, go somewhere and be anonymous and do these stories that have been waiting so long in my mind. Writing about John Wolseley painting in Australia would be one of them. Traveling in Western China would be another. For years I've wanted to write probably three or four stories I think of as *National Geographic* pieces, though I'd want them to have more depth than some of those stories do. I've always wanted to do a story about fabric. About all that clothing that goes to Goodwill and what happens to it. Relatively little of it ends up being clothing for somebody else. Most of it's shipped overseas, where it's used for dozens of different things. So I wanted to look all over the world at what happens to this early invention, weaving—weaving thread together, producing cloth. I'm not so much interested in, you know, certain kinds of cloth, but in its recycling and the

---

*A book Lopez co-edited with Debra Gwartney in 2006.

ways in which cloth is used industrially, where only cotton cloth will work, as in some space vehicles and things like that. But I want to take this simple innovation and follow it all the way out. I'd also like to go back and work with an outfit like United Parcel Service, but this time, instead of flying all over the world the way I did for "Flight," to follow these little trucks out to the end of the little lanes and roads, and build up some sense of what "international" means today. But I have other work to finish first. I do accept some invitations to speak. . . .

TYDEMAN: *So trying to find the appropriate balance . . .*
LOPEZ: Well, I've been trying to do that for years. A lot of writers, especially in these political times, feel their attentions are divided. I just finished reading a set of novels for a prize that Barbara Kingsolver gives out. You spend some of your time doing things that are in service to the community of men and women who write. You just have to do these things. I sometimes long to disappear. But, you know, if you accept invitations and sign contracts, you have no room to complain.

TYDEMAN: *Yes. Did MacDowell* help restore any of this for you?*
LOPEZ: It did. It was remarkable, what happened there. In three weeks I rediscovered what it means to work in the way I want to work. I was in good company, there were wonderful people there, and I came home with a sense of what *Horizon* was about and where I was going with that book. But—please excuse the complaining—I still can't seem to make a period of uninterrupted time in my life in which to write. Like you or anybody else, I walk up to my desk every day and find it full of phone calls to return, messages to answer, somebody's translation questions, somebody wants permission to reprint, this book has to be sent to Korea. . . . Then, you know, there are things like this show, *The Modern West: American Land-*

---

*The MacDowell Colony, founded in Peterborough, New Hampshire, in 1907, provides residency and meals for up to eight weeks for creative individuals engaged in producing enduring works of the imagination.

CONVERSATIONS WITH BARRY LOPEZ

scapes, 1890–1950, which the Museum of Fine Arts, Houston, is putting together that I'm very eager to help with. I'm eager to do all the projects I've got going, but if I don't change *something,* I'm going to be living a life of promising myself I'll get to it next year.

TYDEMAN: *Yes. Sometimes I think you could effectively utilize the skills of some bright young people to help you with organizing or filing or things like that . . .*
LOPEZ: The one thing I wish I had in my life was an assistant.

TYDEMAN: *Yes. That was what I was thinking.*
LOPEZ: It would help me more than anything to have what comes through the door every day organized, for someone to anticipate what my responses are going to be, to make a set of phone calls.

TYDEMAN: *You should get a Texas Tech student who has an internship. Internships can be six months or something like that, and they would actually get some course credit, too.*
LOPEZ: It would take me six months to train somebody.

TYDEMAN: *Yes, you've said that before and now I remember you saying that.*
LOPEZ: If somebody came to work with me, I would have to be assured that they were coming for the long haul.

TYDEMAN: *Long term.*
LOPEZ: Yes. Someone, actually, has written me, somebody highly qualified. She says she'll move to Oregon. I hope if it unfolds I'll know what to do to make it work for both of us.

Art, Activism, and the Biological Fate of Communities

Texas Tech University, Lubbock, Texas
March 24, 2007

WILLIAM E. TYDEMAN: *Barry, during the last week at Texas Tech you've talked about illumination and action.*
BARRY LOPEZ: Yes.

TYDEMAN: *The task of the writer is to illuminate but also the growing necessity is to provide a plan of action.*
LOPEZ: Your question goes to the heart of a problem I am now trying to resolve. In fact, just this morning I was writing this out in my journal, trying to discover the symbols or trains of thought that might help me understand it. As far back as I can remember, I have had questions about the degree to which I should be an activist. As an undergraduate at Notre Dame in the sixties, I felt strongly attracted to the Peace Corps and other humanitarian organizations working in nations that I felt were being forced to pay some sort of price for economic development in the United States. I saw injustice, and I wanted to do something to address the injustice. Now, forty years later, I still feel that impulse, as a writer, and a lack of resolution around it. What I mean by lack of resolution is that I'm not entirely comfortable in either mode, either as a socially engaged writer with no public life, no component of activism in my work, or, at the other extreme, out in public all the time seeking resolutions to some of these injustices, which have just grown larger in the last forty years.

The events following 9/11 and the policies of the Bush presidency have brought into sharp focus the kind of waywardness we're capable of as a country. The aggressive, oblivious pursuit of material wealth at the cost of severe suffering in the rest of the world is perhaps the most profound injustice in the history of international civilization, beginning with England's great expansion of the international slave trade in the sixteenth century. These problems, which of course many others see as well, are difficult to deal with if you're trying to find an appropriate and effective artistic response to what you could understand as a failure of virtue in this country—failed reverence, failed justice, failed courage. By that I mean a general failure in American public life to be courageous in the face of injustice, to pursue justice itself, to revamp a system of education in order to teach reverence rather than a philosophy of acquisition and personal advancement.

In the last few weeks I seem to have arrived at a crossroads in my life. Like many other writers appalled by the savage indifference, the myopic vision, the bullying, the jingoism, the fear-mongering, and the insolence of the Bush administration, I began speaking in public much more frequently after 9/11. Now I feel I've come to the end of that cycle. Whatever work lies ahead, it involves sitting by myself in front of a typewriter. I have a few things to finish up—work with Frank Stewart on two issues of his journal, *Manoa*, dedicated to the theme of reconciliation; a reconciliation ceremony between the Comanche Nation and Texas Tech University; some work with Mercy Corps, an international humanitarian aid organization. I'm also working with a group called Quest for Global Healing to bring people to Hawai'i in 2009 to confer with traditional native Hawaiians in order to provide illumination and discover paths of action, to use your earlier terms.

The deep-seated problems we face in our national disagreements over rights of ownership and the use of natural resources come down to questions of community health and longevity. Government, for the most part, is too beholden to economic interests ever to engage in realistic solutions to these environmental problems. My belief is that the only solutions for us lie with strengthening the emergence of civil society. Civil society works locally to create justice and to *re*-enhance human endeavor with a sense of reverence for life. Its intent is to seek ways to share what belongs to all of us and to marginalize the efforts of governments and businesses to acquire stores of material wealth and then supervise their distribution. Free market capitalism is an experiment, of course, but so is democracy. With the concentration of capital in a very few hands and various forms of serfdom indispensable to "globalization," with so many divisions between the haves and the have-nots—democracy seems incapable of dismantling all this. In the United States, what passes for democracy is a form of governance that concentrates wealth in the hands of a few people and that shows little or no concern for the fate of ordinary people if offering them health care, education, or safety conflicts with economic growth.

What I'm trying to lay out for you here is a generalization. My thoughts are perhaps impulsive, though I can trace the state of frustration that produces them back forty years. My own answer to injustice has been either to absent myself from the world and write a book or an essay or a story, or to fully participate, by coming to Texas Tech, for example, and working on curriculum development and bringing the Comanche Nation into the daily life of the university. I want to do all these things, but I don't have the kind of time to do this work that I had when I was twenty or thirty. More importantly, I want to turn to the manuscripts I still want to write, and away from an involvement with other people and projects. I feel myself being pulled very strongly in recent months into a more private life, toward a concentration on written work instead of activism. Or to use, again, the word you brought up, turning back to whatever passes in my work for illumination. To leave the action to people whose own cycling through their professional lives is leading them into a period of activism. I think my period of activism is coming to an end. I don't say that because I want to abandon that responsibility, but because it's been a long time since I sat down with a very difficult idea and tried to work it out in the form of a book. I feel like I'm coasting a little bit on what I've already done, and I feel a certain illegitimacy in that. I want to go back to the strengths of my work—going to places, meeting people, and trying to be a diligent, thoughtful, respectful reporter. That's what I want to get back to.

TYDEMAN: *You mentioned just a moment ago feeling the sense of getting back to the core strengths of your work. And, yet, I think of the illumination provided in your short story collections* Light Action in the Caribbean *and* Resistance.

LOPEZ: Yes.

TYDEMAN: *The attempt to find the correct distribution between the life of action and the life of contemplation is a central matter for so many writers. However, it sounds like you've already made the decision to give up fiction for the larger project of nonfiction. Am I overreading that?*

LOPEZ: I'm speculating, you know, about what's actually going on with me. I mean, most of us like to think we understand what we're doing, that we have a plan for what we're going to do, but I don't know very many people for whom that is the case. It doesn't work out for most of us. It's been a while since I sat down to write a major piece of nonfiction. *Resistance* is there, *Light Action in the Caribbean*. I'm glad I did that work. I'd like to continue writing fiction, but those pieces, even in *Resistance*, where all the stories are linked together, its scale is smaller than that of *Arctic Dreams*. I want to return to work on a larger scale, and for me now that feels like nonfiction. I daydream about a theme in fiction I can pursue in depth and at length, at least at the length of a novella, but what's in the foreground for me right now is a work of nonfiction in which I can use rhythms less attenuated than those of an essay. My plan for the coming months is to work on a couple of essays, autobiographical pieces, and so reintroduce myself to what I was trying to do in the eighties with the shorter work that preceded *Arctic Dreams*.

Something to emphasize here in talking about activism and whether I should take a step back is that these decisions are complicated for me by two issues. One is that, as time goes on, I feel a stronger and stronger sense of the importance of the biological fate of human communities. The second is that we are living in a time the like of which humanity has never seen. It's always dangerous to suggest that your time is like no other time in history, but, with global climate change, and, just to pick one thing, flooding the environment with synthetic hormones, we don't know what we've gotten ourselves into as a species. We know that fresh water is in shorter and shorter supply every day. We know that the carbon-fueled economy that has developed in the United States and other "first world" nations is not something that can be sustained. If you take the long view that an evolutionary biologist would, wondering what's in store for *Homo sapiens*, you don't have to be a fatalist or a misanthrope to say that the possibility here around issues of genetic damage and diminishing supplies of water doesn't look good. It doesn't look good around increased solar radiation and climate change, knowing that these things can't be fixed overnight, and that we may already be many years into an irreversible situation. So, deciding whether to write, to separate myself from the fray and write, or to remain an activist, I'm not making that decision against a backdrop of believing we have a benign future ahead. In other words, I can make an argument with myself that all I should do from now till my time is up is whatever I can to motivate people, to ensure that some number of human beings get through the Venturi tube, that there's a possibility for this organism on the other side. But, frankly, I feel I'm living in a time of entrenched and catastrophic ignorance. The number of people who don't want to consider some other way, for whom science is an enemy, is terrifying. The degree to which religious dogma has affected the discourse about human fate is chilling. It's not a matter of asking whether one should write . . .

TYDEMAN: *Yes.*

LOPEZ: I believe strongly in the idea of individual artistic vision and in following that vision, no matter what others are doing, but I don't see that we're in a situation like that now. Can we afford artistic ambition that is indifferent to human life? The stakes now are very high. You can imagine, for example, that a painter born today might not ever have the wherewithal to follow an artistic life, to produce much art before her life is over. Like anyone else, artists may find themselves fighting daily for food and water. These are realities that we have to contend with, and about which we are in psychotic denial.

TYDEMAN: *Would you talk about your understanding of indigenous knowledge and how it might help with these problems?*

LOPEZ: The first thing I should say is that I don't believe so-called advanced cultures, like Western culture, are bad or evil and that traditional cultures are superior. It's more productive to posit that the headlong progress of Western civilization has created major problems for many other cultures. If the idea is to survive or, better, to live fully and well, it seems to me an intelligent person would ask what it is that these marginalized cultures are doing—some of them have been around for tens of thousands of years—that has ensured their survival? And what are *we* doing that is not in our own best interests if our goal, too, is to survive? You can't walk into a traditional village and pick a person at random and discover a reservoir of wisdom that will guide you. All traditional cultures have within them, at their core, groups of people we call elders or senior people. These would be people who have led extremely attentive lives and who've made it their business to listen to what those who came before them had to say about what makes a good way of life. We no longer have that component in Western culture. Our tendency is to move cautious or questioning people out of the way and to regard the past as less than the present. We're so devoted to the idea of progress, it doesn't normally occur to us that someone from the past would know better than we know in the present. Their way of thinking about wisdom and knowledge is foreign to us. We're so wedded to the idea of improved technologies that we've fallen into the habit of thinking about improved forms of government or improved forms of education. What I argue for here is a different kind of people around the table when we're making decisions that affect everyone on the planet. It's a kind of eerie miracle to me that traditional wisdom, earth-based as opposed to text-based wisdom, is still vital in cultures all over the world, despite the ways in which those cultures have been persecuted. To my knowledge, people in most of these cultures are still willing to share. They've only asked for some space at the table, which should be theirs anyway.

It's not news to anyone that the United States is institutionally compromised when it comes to dealing equitably with American citizens because of entrenched racism. You might learn in an American high school how Japanese citizens were treated in the internment camps during the Second World War. But you're not going to hear about the Chinese laborers who were just killed, murdered, when work on the western railroads was finished. You're not going to hear about Washita or Sand Creek, about Bear River in Idaho, about Palo Duro Canyon and Tule Canyon here in Texas. The genocide directed against peoples in the Americas is not something most Americans want to hear about, any more than they want to be reminded of slavery. Americans generally prefer to believe that America is the land of the free and the home of the brave, which is no more true of us than it is of some other nations. We're not a free people. We live in economic serfdom, and our ability to effect legislative change through our vote is little better than what is possible in some de facto dictatorships, where one or another ideologue comes to power and, no matter the form of "democratic" government, puts to work an undemocratic ideology within the framework of that democracy. I'm not unusual among American writers who have been trying to pay attention to what peoples all over the world have been saying about justice, about the missing conversation in America.

····

I've said this elsewhere, but the term "nature writing" is an inadequate and often inappropriate term for a kind of literature that addresses injustice and hierarchy. The term marginalizes the work. For me, a certain strain of feminist writing, a certain strain of civil rights writing, and a certain strain of writing about the relationship between nature and culture are all embedded in the same impulse, a sense of outrage about injustice in the United States.

TYDEMAN: *So part of the task of educational institutions is to invite people to the table who bring a perspective and an alternative way of thinking about the problems that we face.*

LOPEZ: Yes. Particularly now when, to say this again, the threat is so big and the stakes are so high. I find it helpful to understand that when we gather to talk about these problems, we often talk about them as though they were *out* there somewhere, and that we need to mount an adequate defense, when in fact most of the problems we're talking about have already arrived, decades ago. Asking how we're going to defend ourselves against them can become an exercise in despair. In other words, if you've been unknowingly infected by a virus and years later you learn this virus is on the loose, and you begin discussing how to deal with it, and then the doctor tells you the virus is already in your body, that's a recipe for despair. Where I find a sense of hope is to say yes, the prospects are terrifying and, yes, the trouble has been here for a long time, but the human desire to effectively address the problems is also entrenched, and it, too, has been here for a long time. So for someone just developing the courage to confront some of these things, like ozone depletion or the possibility that the Gulf Stream will cease to flow or disappear altogether in the coming decade, to know others have been working on these issues for a long while takes some of the chill out.

I used to find it irritating when books about environmental problems carried listings at the back of all the organizations you could contact to go to work on these problems. These books seemed like manuals to me, like manifestos, which of course they were. What I missed was a coherent underlying philosophy, the sense that these problems were all rooted in injustice, in unjust relations with the Earth and with each other. I wanted the response of the outraged reader to be linked more strongly to social and political issues, to the emergence of a new natural philosophy. But I've come to realize that illumination must be accompanied by action if there is to be any real change. Environmental books today list organizations to contact or send you to a website, and you can begin your investigation. Electronic databases allow you to search the web for all kinds of information, though, again, they don't supply a coherent narrative. It seems to me that if a book can supply a narrative, and then in the appendices direct you to some databases, you will have a useful matrix in your mind—a philosophy—that allows you to organize and select among the material you find on the web. To go to the web to try to learn the shape of the peril is an exercise in frustration. So, in a work of nonfiction, I'm thinking more often now that I want to have some kind of reference at the end of the book that will lead people to the information they require to form a good plan of action. I'm very much in favor of some things that I've seen recently, in *National Geographic* for example, where an article about one or another kind of difficulty has a little box at the end telling you what you might do. Not whom to write a check to, but what it is you could actually do, now that you grasp the problem.

TYDEMAN: *As an extension of what we've just been talking about, you've had occasion to prod our thinking with the work of several people whom you've found particularly useful in sorting through these questions about action and social justice. How have their efforts helped provide a framework for understanding?*

LOPEZ: Well, I just recently read Paul Hawken's *Blessed Unrest*, and I felt Paul was very successful in making clear what the movement toward civil society is all about and what the foundation of a hopeful stance, a hopeful frame of mind, might actually be. He's clear in the beginning of the book that what we face is terrifying, and that we can either stand paralyzed or we can act. The action he advocates is local action, staying in touch with or getting in touch with people who are acting locally, and recognizing that other people all over the world are doing the same. In the aggregate, this kind of civil action is our only hope against self-serving governments and self-aggrandizing business. I don't mean to condemn business—when a civilization reaches the scale of the one we're living in, some forms of business are necessary and good. But there is a destructive, malicious element in international commerce in particular that seems to be beyond the ability of good people in or out of the business world to control. Most of us are appalled by the behavior of certain large corporations, their cavalier dismissal of the principles of democracy, their unwillingness to pay taxes, their indifference to the injustices they perpetuate. These entities, which any sane and just person would want to see dismantled, have a life of their own, and they are often stronger than the individuals who want to come to grips with them ethically.

In Seattle in 1999 you had a mixed group of protesters on the streets during World Trade Organization meetings, vocally objecting to injustices that WTO representatives seemed to think were just part of doing business, a kind of collateral damage. If the State of California decides that it wants less automobile pollution in the air and passes state regulations to that effect, and those regulations are declared null and void by WTO—they can do that—people would argue, rightfully, that the unilateral action of WTO is unjust, simply for public health reasons. Most Americans are not well informed about the extraordinary power WTO has, to make the world a safer place for big business. Significant numbers of men and women in big business, I have to believe, are mortified by what business is capable of doing, but they are powerless to act. Protesters and social activists have everything to gain by working in concert with these people, by making common cause with them in bringing this beast under control.

It's not just business that needs to meet the expectations of citizens, it's our rampant technologies, the most salient example of which is the computer. The computer fits in our lives like a spoiled child, always demanding, always getting. We're so dazzled by these new technologies, so seduced by their potential, that we repeat business's mantras about service and benefits to society. Control over these technologies—discipline—doesn't occur to us. And those who advocate control are treated in a smug and angry way as Luddites, as people who are too cautious, too unenlightened, not visionary enough. The testy defense of these technologies by proponents is the reaction of schoolyard bullies. If there is no plan of containment for the technologies we develop, the technologies will inevitably cause harm. Once linked to the massive engine of American consumerism, the situation can become hopeless. Like any other addiction, consumerism sustains itself through denial, sometimes breathtakingly elaborate. I think our call should be as citizen resisters, in the same way that the French Underground resisted the goals of the Nazi Party in France. There is, of course, resistance in the United States and there is also a body of written work—novels, poems, essays—that I would call the writing of resistance. In the past, I have said I wanted my work to be part of a Literature of Hope. What I would say today is that I want my work to be part of a Literature of Resistance. The resistance is to the activities of government and business that perpetuate injustice, that institutionalize the hierarchies that compromise human and planetary health.

I want to say that I seem to have posited an "us/them" frame of reference here, which I don't mean to. I have felt a shift in myself recently as a writer, a movement toward work that is more overtly about injustice, and I'm teetering here on the high wire, trying to discover an approach that is not self-righteous, not self-satisfied, but vulnerable, questing, compassionate.

TYDEMAN: *Well, this makes me think of the tension between knee-jerk reaction and active listening. Not labeling someone the enemy, I think is the phrase that you've used. My question is how does one accomplish that? You want to bring together the people who represent these diverse perspectives, you want them to be part of the conversation. And yet so often, we'll expend enormous energy in denunciation and diatribe.*

LOPEZ: When I have advocated for not spending time identifying and then pursuing and killing an enemy, what I'm trying to say is, the enemy is always a distraction, and the enemy will never disappear. There will always be a threat of some sort—an "enemy"—when you're trying to pursue a life that is just and courageous and reverent. So the idea that you must defeat the enemy is unenlightened. The amount of energy that goes into the defeat of an enemy is energy that would be better spent in doing something that makes the enemy irrelevant. That's what the movement toward civil society is about. Instead of revolting with guns in the street and acts of terrorism directed against business and government, you concentrate instead on making common cause at the local level. You give up the idea that you're going to develop some kind of policy or approach that will be acceptable to people all over the world. That's not going to happen. But the creation of just conditions in many local arenas eventually adds up to the same thing. It's just arriving at justice from the bottom up, not the top down. Globalization is an attempt to make money at the expense of an anonymous world. The idea that we can all have one religion or one language, and that one system of economics will work for all, depersonalizes everyone. It's a child's plan. The striving of individual human beings should take place within the context of their own cultures and be directed toward building beautiful relations in those cultures. Again, by focusing on the development of good relations in the local community, you in effect create a world of beautiful localities.

I heard someone last night say that what the federal government needs to do is to develop policies to be administered through the Department of Agriculture that would lower the number of diseases that now attack American forests. It would be better if local people took care of local trees. And one way you take care of local trees is to make sure there is diversity in the community of trees. When Dutch elm disease moves through, if you don't have anything but elms you're in trouble. If you had a lot of *other* kinds of trees, it would be like someone in the family getting cancer and maybe dying, but the family doesn't die.

Our predilection for monoculture makes good business sense, but it's to our detriment as human beings. We know this. We know what to do. We know that we need to act locally and not be convening international meetings to develop international policies for everyone to follow. I think this is true even with something like whaling. The International Whaling Commission is having trouble now getting some nations to agree to stop whaling, but the enforcement pressure it can bring to bear is minimal. These are decisions that have to be made by individuals in Norway, or in Iceland, or in Japan. We can't meet somewhere and say, okay, this is what everyone has to do. Where scientific information is at a premium, we can meet and have scientists from different parts of the world share this information, but we can also do that electronically, and meeting at big conferences keeps our problems in the realm of the abstract. Mass media, if they choose, can catch up on what's going on at conferences and report the news to nonspecialists. But the master-of-the-world daydream that people like Mr. Bush have—strong men, operating from the top down—these are not tenable plans.

I must say that the last few years have been years of struggle for me when it comes to keeping faith. I used to feel that all you really needed to create the necessary changes was the five or ten percent of people who were paying attention. I don't know if that's true anymore. I see the power of institutions, the way they gravitate toward a dangerous kind of mediocrity, as a strong indication that large-scale institutions can't ever be effective. The environmental issues that need to be addressed simply can't be addressed, in the time available, by institutions—by federal governments, by banks, by big business. They are too timid, too mired in an antiquated Western folklore of superiority, too wedded to the idea that any regulation signals their end. The only successful ways in which these large problems are being addressed is through the sharing of information and the sharing of ways of acting that are effective. No doubt Muhammad Yunus–type banking, some municipal governments, and some small businesses are of inestimable help here.

TYDEMAN: *You've also said that one of your concerns is learning to talk about generosity in perhaps a darker way. Do you mean the unintended consequences of generosity?*

LOPEZ: Well, this is a tricky area, and something I'm on the verge of writing about. When I was nineteen or twenty, I was eager to contribute to just causes through the Peace Corps and other, similar organizations. I wanted to right wrongs in the world. It didn't occur to me then that institutionalized compassion is as risky a venture as institutionalized corporate exploitation. What I mean is that if you go into a foreign country and develop supplies of clean water but don't address the underlying cause of so much contaminated water, then your actions might ultimately be considered futile. A lot of philanthropy—this is where it gets dangerous—a lot of philanthropy and doing good in the world is carried out by people who have both a sense of compassion and a sense of responsibility driven by generalized feelings of guilt. The doing of good assuages that anxiety and the pain a person might have in his or her soul, and I respect that. But, to help victims of globalization and not, at the same time, do all you can to undermine and dismantle the machinery of globalization, the way it crushes communities and ruins landscapes to grab natural resources and market share, is, ultimately, to lead a life of neutrality.

TYDEMAN: *So again, the assumption that you are doing good without understanding the larger implications.*

LOPEZ: Yes. And I think people who have dedicated their entire careers to humanitarian aid would tell you—maybe not for quotation, but in private conversation—that, yes, there is a danger of falling in love with your own work, and of growing comfortable with the root causes of poverty, famine, and disease, the very reasons your work is necessary. I say this is a dangerous topic to address because I can't condemn out of hand the very work I myself want to participate in. I believe, however, that to minister to those who are damaged by an international quest for wealth and power and not to criticize the entities that create these problems is, in my mind, to be paralyzed, to stand frightened and intimidated. There are many legitimate and laudable reasons for doing humanitarian work, and, as I said, I'm just now on the verge of exploring it. In the coming months I'll try to get myself face-to-face with some of these situations in the Middle East and in Central and Southeast Asia. I want to go into diaspora camps, where some people don't even have a name anymore, where everything has been stripped away. They're just trying to get enough protein and water to be able to move out of the sun. I'll make mistakes in posing my questions, I'll see my preconceptions fall apart, but it's important for me to pursue this now. I'd rather fall on my face doing this kind of research than live in a world of intellectualized emotions.

I don't have a save-the-world point of view or goal, I just want to contribute to the general effort, to bring beauty and grace and light, if you will, where there is now cruelty and darkness and spiritual ugliness. I don't have much to lose here. I sit at the typewriter or deliver a talk if I'm asked. I contribute with a group of people sitting around a table toward shaping the things we're all determined to do. In general, for a writer to try to tell people what to think is just—I don't want to say that it's wrong, but it is not my way. I believe most people can make informed decisions, they just need useful, pertinent, dependable information and to be treated like people who can be trusted where the fate of the community is concerned.

I can tell you something. All my adult life, as I've said, I've felt pulled in two directions—toward writing and toward humanitarian aid, toward doing work on behalf of others, and this tension has affected the way I understand literature. Literature grows out of storytelling, and storytelling evolved, I believe, as a social impulse rather than an art, what we would today identify as the unfolding of an individual, artistic vision. Even if a Paleolithic storyteller had a distinctive style and great craft, it seems to me that early storytelling still would have embodied an ethical relationship with the listener. The storyteller would have been aware of the listener's fate, and aware that he or she shared that fate. So when I talk about contemporary literature, I tend to use the term in a strict and narrow way. For me, literature has three salient characteristics. The writer's love of language drives a distinct style and reveals an artistic vision. The story itself illuminates some aspect of the modern dilemma. And, third, its revelations are about us. It's not about the writer, especially the writer as avatar. In asserting this, I'm raising large and contentious questions, and my overall approach might sound insufferably elitist. But my point is this: not everyone is an artist. And not every artist is successful in every artistic endeavor. Art does something special. It carries with it today the residue of Paleolithic ceremony and magic. And, historically, in terrible times, it was ceremony and magic that gave people the psychic means to endure, to survive. I'm not attempting to set up special quarters here for "gifted writers" or trying to argue their status as an elite corps. I'm saying that with the commercialization of book publishing, with widespread indifference to the reader's fate, the relegation of the reader to the status of customer or consumer, and with the neurotic quest, particularly in America, for celebrity and special status, literature has suffered as an art. Commerce and fashion—this I know is a ho-hum observation—have compromised all the arts in modern times. My anxiety, my argument, is that we are at risk of losing what art does, or of having its effective range catastrophically reduced, at a time when humanity is severely threatened biologically and chemically. When we most need story—not information, not rhetoric, not entertainment, not promotion—we find that story—the elevating and healing event, the exchange of emotions we call story—has been sent to Siberia. The stories most readily available to us are products. The life-sustaining magic, the reincorporation of ourselves into the river of life—generally, that is not there now.

TYDEMAN: *I've recently come across the work of Eliot Eisner, who talks about the marginalization of the arts in our culture and how we see art education as peripheral. He argues that art carries with it the possibility of the transformation of consciousness. That in fact this is the special power of art. With all the collaboration you have done with visual and performing artists, does that resonate for you?*

LOPEZ: Very much so. I would say that it's more often the case that someone changes the way we see the world because of their exposure to art than because of their exposure to rational thought. We strive for sound arguments because we're a culture that really values rational thinking. We tend to believe, for example, that if you can get a group of people together at a table and explain how atmospheric chemistry is creating global climate change, that people will, as we say, see the light. In their personal lives and in their career lives they will do whatever they can to effect a change. But that doesn't happen. The metaphorical stories of the Bible are affecting, of course, but they are rooted in archetypal feelings that predate Christianity. When God knocks Saul from his horse on the road to Damascus, Saul's conversion is caused by spiritual not rational revelation. This is a way we have of reminding ourselves—in story—that it's not rational thought that causes the kind of dramatic change humanity needs now—I'm using the word "need" because the survival of *Homo sapiens* for me is a need [*laughs*]. I recall many moments of heightened awareness in my life that didn't necessarily change the way I saw the world, but they made life itself, its value, more compelling, and not a one of them had anything to do with rational thought. You can't, for example, reason your way to love. "Love" is a frequently misused and, for some, a naive term. The essence of love is reciprocity. It's the state in which waves of energy move in opposite directions but in parallel along the same path. It's antiphony, a calling back and forth. It's the expression of a reciprocated relationship. And it is precisely these "loving" relationships that create the literal and figurative entity we call an ecosystem. The effort toward justice is an effort toward more perfect love. The effort to improve relationships, in all realms, is an effort to create a more loving, a more just, environment.

TYDEMAN: *But to create that loving environment, to create love, we must have trust. And to trust is to make ourselves vulnerable.*

LOPEZ: People in a culture like ours are disaffected in part because we find it so difficult to establish intimate relations with other people, with ideas, with the physical world. Intimate experience hinges on a willingness to be vulnerable. You can't have intimacy without vulnerability, and, to my way of thinking, the reluctance to be vulnerable to the world grows out of a failure to trust, as you imply. We are a people longing, I think, for intimacy, but you can't have intimacy without vulnerability, and you can't have vulnerability without trust, and in our commercially driven society where there is such an emphasis on personal advancement it's difficult to trust. It occurred to me recently that one of the hallmarks of achieving a state of intimacy is the blossoming of a generalized sense of hope. In a moment of great intimacy you become hopeful, but it's not about something that can be put into concrete terms, like feeling you're going to win the lottery or that your sister's cancer operation will be successful. It's the intensification of a belief that things will work out. This would suggest that a good way to steer clear of despair and denial is to seek moments of intimacy. The pursuit of intimate knowing is emerging for me now as an antidote to general despair about the human condition.

TYDEMAN: *Intimate knowing?*
LOPEZ: Yes, intimate knowing, a kind of inquiring reciprocity. When I was walking across the campus this morning I found a beetle. Its life had expired. It was on its back on the sidewalk. I squatted down to examine it and in my mind I asked, "Who were you?" and "What was the cause of this?" I tried to enter into a state in which the beetle was not an object. To initiate some kind of relationship with what was left of the beetle is, for me, a kind of practice, an effort to stay in touch with the world. To stay intimate. To sense the great enterprise of a university around me, thirty thousand students, and in the middle of it a life that's passed away, contextualizes, to use that emotionally barren term, what it means to have an education. You can get an education in the classroom, but the education in the classroom is of no use, I believe, unless you are able to enter into some sort of relationship with something as apparently innocuous as the dead beetle.

TYDEMAN: *And isn't that also the core of indigenous ways of knowledge, existing in relationship with all other forms, be they animate or inanimate?*
LOPEZ: To me one of the most striking differences between indigenous cultures and our culture is their love of attachment and our fear of it. In traditional cultures, people strive to be included in a set of relationships, to ground their identity in a set of relationships. In a culture like ours, the tendency is to regard all relationships as provisional, as

potentially stultifying, to identify instead with the growth of the self, not with a set of layered relationships. We value what you might call a right to exploit, and we're reluctant to give it up because in the hands of strong people, willful people, exploitation creates material wealth. Traditional cultures, in my experience, are puzzled by why you would give up a feeling of being wanted, of having a reciprocated place in the world, in order to secure material wealth.

TYDEMAN: *That's interesting, because wisdom books like The Course in Miracles talk about this essential tension—it's love or it's fear. Why has organized religion failed to embrace this ambiguity? You grew up in the Catholic Church, yet you made a decision not to consciously break with the church but to explore other traditions.*

LOPEZ: Yes. My own tradition finally seemed narrow. I know far too little about Hinduism or Islam or Buddhism to speak with any authority, but organized religion seems to me to be a codification of spirituality, and the fear we discover in organized religion, and that we associate with fundamentalism, is the fear of being wrong. What people too heavily invested in organized religion are afraid of is process. Darwinian evolution in biology is about process, about change that is unpredictable and that has no endpoint. Process theology is based on the ongoing process of knowing God. My principal difficulties with organized religion have to do with the reduced role given to the imagination. I'm not saying someone can't create a beautiful spiritual life within the context of organized religion, but it's not something that has worked for me. I guess, like most artists and writers, I find the God-like in the realm of the imagination rather than in the realm of the intellect. And for me as an individual, the realm of God is most often experienced in a numinous encounter with landscape. That's where it's usually most intense, walking through a landscape and encountering an animal or weather of some sort and suddenly I'm in a world of a blinding light. I couldn't find a home for that kind of approach to God in traditional Christianity. Traditional Christianity has a strong component of self-righteousness and a strong impulse, as in Islam or Mormonism, toward missionizing. It's a colonial impulse. The United States proselytizes for an international conversion to its system of economics, other people proselytize for international conversion to their religion. It's not simply a failure of justice, it speaks to a failure of imagination, or, to use a Catholic metaphor, to a fall from grace.

TYDEMAN: *We've had a conversation here at Texas Tech about the important distinction you've drawn between morality and ethics and how we're often guilty of confusing the two. How might ethical systems help us in facing the great challenges we've got in the twenty-first century?*

LOPEZ: I'm not a philosopher, and I use those terms—ethical, moral—perhaps incorrectly or imprecisely. I would certainly defer to a formally trained philosopher here who wanted to say I've actually misunderstood something. That said, for me, there is a difference between moral behavior and ethical behavior. Moral behavior is judged according to a set of laws laid down in a text, like the Qur'an or the Bible. Ethical behavior is judged according to the precepts of a secular philosophy. Ethical behavior can be—and very often is—moral, but some ethical actions may be judged immoral by those adhering strictly to the tenets of one religion or another. One way in which morals and ethics differ is that in an unprecedented situation, while an ethical course of action might be clear, a moral course of action might not be. It might take a long time to shape the threat into something the authoritative text recognizes. You can discover an ethics that applies in an unprecedented situation because it's based on philosophy, not on texts. Insisting on moral values in a democracy, therefore, is a contradiction. Different religions have different moral codes. A democracy, strictly speaking, must be based on *ethical* values. That means you have to be willing to enter into perplexing or even "immoral" situations in order to discover a way to eliminate the cruelty or injustice inherent in that situation. The search for moral behavior will always run aground if there's more than one religion in the room. With the search for ethical behavior, it's reasonable to assume that people with differing religious backgrounds can agree on what is ethical. I think it's more productive in a world like ours, where people have different religious traditions, to seek common ethical ground rather than common moral ground. These terms are used interchangeably by most people, but I like to preserve the distinction because I think it's helpful. If you keep the focus on what is ethical rather than on what is moral, no one has to compromise their faith to come into agreement.

TYDEMAN: *Barry, to shift our focus a bit, one of your earliest pieces on Native American philosophy was "The American Indian Mind," which was published in Quest in 1978. If you were pressed to give the origins of your concern with indigenous peoples, and the importance of cross-cultural understanding, would you say that Barre Toelken served as a catalyst for your thinking?*
LOPEZ: Yes. Without question.

TYDEMAN: *You have written about being introduced to a wider array of thinkers and intellectuals through Toelken. Seemingly, that created the intellectual spark for your exploration.*
LOPEZ: It did. I got a very good liberal education at Notre Dame, but it was parochial. The University of Oregon, where I met Toelken, didn't provide the same caliber of education Notre Dame did, but I discovered in Toelken a teacher who affected my whole life as a writer.

TYDEMAN: *And would there be a direct relationship between that experience and your decision early on to work on the Coyote tales and stories?*
LOPEZ: I first learned about the Trickster figure in class with Toelken. I was immediately intrigued by what Jung called a character who was the embodiment of undifferentiated good and evil. Discovering that character in Toelken's class on American folklore opened the door for me onto Native American thought. It was the kind of thing I never would have encountered at Notre Dame.

TYDEMAN: *Right. I'd like to talk about your collection of Trickster tales, Giving Birth to Thunder, Sleeping with His Daughter. It's the most misunderstood of your books. In 1978, people came to the book with a particular agenda that didn't permit them to understand your larger intent. Occasionally I still see complaints about the stories, without an understanding of your pedagogical intent.*

LOPEZ: My intent was to make the general reader aware of Coyote as a central figure in Paleolithic story, a character who has come down to us in North America—as a colonial people, as Euro-Americans—in the form of the various Trickster figures found in Native American oral tradition. The traditions differ, but the Trickster figure seems to be something deeply embedded in human consciousness. When I encountered the Trickster figure in Toelken's class, I went immediately to the library and began reading Trickster stories. The more I read, the more excited I became about the character, and about what his behavior said about the human psyche. I'm not an anthropologist, I'm not a literary scholar. I was interested in creating versions of the stories that were evocative, accessible, human. I think a few of the early reviews took me to task for not doing what I wasn't trying to do.

TYDEMAN: *Yes.*

LOPEZ: It's sometimes the case with reviews that people argue for the book they would have written and ignore the book in front of them. In some sense, I suppose—I was twenty-three at the time—I was trying to take the Trickster stories away from scholars and return them to the world of ordinary humans. I wanted to translate the Latin euphemisms, for example, to actually use images that scholarly editors considered offensive. I had no ambition—or qualification—to attempt to write a scholarly book. I admire scholarship as I admire science. When scholars and scientists claim the truth is theirs alone, though, that's when I politely slip out of the room.

TYDEMAN: *When you began writing for* Harper's *and other major magazines, you experienced the tensions of editorial control. It seems to me that that's an issue that anybody who's chosen to make a living from writing has got to wrestle with almost continually.*

LOPEZ: I used to think in terms of two major challenges in magazine work. One was the creation of the piece, the research and writing, the other was the successful publication of the piece—copyediting, fact checking. Today, I think in terms of three difficulties: the creation of the piece, the protection of the piece in its original form, and its publication. When I was writing for *Harper's* in the eighties and early nineties, I worked so diligently to polish the story before submission that it was unusual for anyone to do more than change a word or two. You accepted it or you didn't. Somewhere in the nineties, magazines seemed to enter a phase in which more people wanted their fingerprints on the story. With the advent of this kind of group editing, and with the development of electronic editing, writers had to start dealing with a manuscript that, in some ways, was owned by no one. The writer provided an original manuscript much in the way a screenwriter provides an initial screenplay. When all was said and done, the published version might be something you didn't feel you'd actually written. I'm no more interested in that experience than a painter is interested in having a gallery owner change a painting so it'll sell more quickly. If I were to start out today as a freelance writer, I'd have to have a very different idea of what it means to discover your voice as a writer. And I wouldn't do well, because I'd rather fail on my own terms than succeed on someone else's. To succeed on somebody else's terms would mean using the work simply to create a byline and a check. For me, ethically, it shows disrespect for the whole enterprise, the history of storytelling.

TYDEMAN: *I could see how that is. Technology makes that a greater and greater challenge.*

LOPEZ: I have always said that I work for people, not institutions, as a writer. Another way to say this is that I work for an editor, not a magazine. I'm glad to respond to editorial direction from an editor who's made an effort to understand the situation out of which the manuscript came. I am impatient with arbitrary or uninformed editing, with editing for the sake of editing, or with edits meant to make my voice more detached, more cynical. All of that represents to me a capitulation to the desiderata of commerce.

TYDEMAN: *But to make the transition from magazine work to the larger work of books, my sense is that you've been unusually fortunate in the editors with whom you've worked.*

LOPEZ: Yes.

TYDEMAN: *The relationship for the most part has proved very productive for you and for your audience.*

LOPEZ: I've been very fortunate to have good editors. But it's important to note that I didn't come to writing as a graduate of a university writing program, where people often hold writing for commercial magazines at arm's length. I started off writing nonfiction for magazines in which my own point of view didn't count for anything. I had to provide clear, cogent information about an event, a person, a thing, if I was to make a living. As far as developing a voice as a writer goes, I was very fortunate that, from time to time, I could find a home for more personal pieces, and that I met editors who encouraged good work, who insisted on it.

I don't think of writing as a career, I think of it as a way of life. So, earlier in our talk, when I said that I feel as if I'm at a crossroads with the amount of activism I've been involved in, on the one hand, and sitting by myself at the typewriter on the other, I have to say that each is an expression of this way of life. But at this point, when I am feeling an excess of one and an absence of the other, to regain a sense of well-being I have to go back to being more of a writer and less of an activist.

TYDEMAN: *To find the right balance.*

LOPEZ: Right. Someone once joked that they could use my professional history selectively to create an impression of me as a literary writer or as a professional writer, a popular writer, either way. Applying labels, you know, puts the emphasis on the writer, when the more useful emphasis would be on the story. Did the story help? Did it work? My long-term interest has always been in a story written for the sake of the reader. I take pleasure in writing the story, and it's gratifying to be told that the writing succeeded, but serving the reader has always been an important component of what I write. And I guess a thought that follows from that is that I am suspicious of any writer's claiming to possess something that others need to know. I'm suspicious of that in myself. If your work comes into some form of public prominence, and you accept a lot of invitations to speak in public, I think you can become obsessed with your own importance and lose the ability to relate to a shared human fate.

TYDEMAN: *I wanted to bring up the origins of much of what you're talking about. At Notre Dame you began early on to involve yourself in journalistic endeavors and radio and in publishing. I know Focus Michiana was a journal that you helped found and worked on. What were the origins of your journalistic and radio work at Notre Dame?*

LOPEZ: I was the only kid in my New York City prep school who had grown up in the West, in California, and who had family in the American South, in Alabama and Georgia. In the way of all high school communities, I was both given credit for that and made the butt of jokes because of it. My classmates regarded me as someone from California, not New York, even though I was born in Westchester County and lived in Mamaroneck, just outside the city, until I was three. In the writing I did back then, when I was fifteen or sixteen, I found myself trying to interpret the agricultural life of California or the rural life of Alabama for a New York audience. How could I get at these things that seemed striking and engaging and worth knowing, for an audience that didn't know anything about them? So, perhaps the origin of my work lies with those early pieces. When I got to Notre Dame, I don't know why I gravitated toward radio, but I got involved in radio and theater as forms of storytelling, probably. I had a program director, a person who determined the kind of show you would host on the radio station, who gave me free rein, so I was able to write scripts for a show called *Precipice*. These were my attempts to write in a narrative or discursive form while getting some emotional support from music, to explore ideas that, to my seventeen-year-old mind, took us out to the edge of knowing. I guess the term today would be "cutting edge" or something like that. The attempt was to create an engaging story through a combination of music and language.

I never got involved with the university's newspaper or its weekly magazine, and the few pieces I submitted to the undergraduate literary magazine, *The Juggler*, were summarily returned with nasty, condescending notes. So, my tentative efforts at Notre Dame to become part of the literary scene were a failure, and the opportunities I had to work as a journalist there were never attractive enough. But . . .

TYDEMAN: *I'm sorry, they were not attractive to you?*
LOPEZ: I wasn't attracted to the deadline situation in journalism.

TYDEMAN: *Oh, I see, writing that didn't allow you to develop the story more fully, which journalism majors . . .*
LOPEZ: We didn't have a journalism major, we had a Department of Communication Arts, which was the center of professionally oriented, writerly activity at Notre Dame—writing for radio or the theater or writing journalism.

TYDEMAN: *I see.*
LOPEZ: The first pieces I had the courage to send out to magazines, in 1966, when I was a senior, were short stories. And that element from my high school days—trying to explain the unknown to the reader, to explore something the reader was probably not aware of—was at the core of those stories. One magazine I began submitting to was *Ave Maria*, a Catholic magazine with leftist views published at Notre Dame. Maybe it was because the magazine was near to hand or because my roommate during my senior year was an editor there, but that's how I began an association with the magazine that published some of my earliest works. I had the normal fixations a young man who'd grown up in the West might have—cars, camping, ranch life. I went on to write about some of those subjects for *Popular Mechanics* and *Popular Science*. I was also writing about the environment for half a dozen magazines. And somewhere around that time, *North American Review* began taking short stories and travel pieces from me.

TYDEMAN: *You began writing for them in the mid-seventies, am I right about that?*
LOPEZ: I'd have to look at the card catalog, maybe 1974 . . .

TYDEMAN: *Was* "My Horse" *one of those early pieces?*
LOPEZ: Yes, *"My Horse"* was an early essay about traveling. I did another piece for *North American Review* in 1974 about rodeo cowboys, called "Going Down with the Bulls," and a couple of other things. I say "for" them, but this was all freelance work. I wasn't being asked by

anyone to work on assignment. That kind of thing was still in the future. I'm not sure how much fiction I wrote for *North American Review* in the beginning, but Robley Wilson, the editor there, was the first editor to take seriously my effort to write literary prose, both fiction and nonfiction. And then came an extended period of work with Lewis Lapham at *Harper's*, though he never became interested in my fiction.

TYDEMAN: *One of the things, Barry, we've not talked about is your involvement in athletics. You were a high school athlete and participated in a number of sports. You also played soccer at Notre Dame?*
LOPEZ: For two years, yeah.

TYDEMAN: *When you look back, what if anything did you take away from your sporting activities?*
LOPEZ: To never lose sight of the importance of the body. I love intensity and exertion, and the sports that attracted me were ones like soccer and basketball, where there's not much opportunity for rest. It's constant movement. I also ran the 100-yard dash and relay races in high school. University life offered me a certain attractive invitation to come indoors, but I was wary. Staying outdoors meant staying in my body, which meant playing soccer for another couple of years. Looking back, I can see that many of the topics or places I've chosen to write about demanded research that required physical exertion. I often feel as intense a pleasure in physical exploration as I do in cerebral exploration, and sometimes I'm writing about the landscape between the two.

TYDEMAN: *Interesting. When you were at Notre Dame and played soccer for two years, was that intercollegiate soccer?*
LOPEZ: Yes. We were a club, we played other university clubs. We played some of the real powerhouses back then. St. Louis, for example. I've forgotten where all we traveled to. It wasn't an intramural sport.

TYDEMAN: *Right. And why only two years?*
LOPEZ: I don't know. You move on, you know? I mean, I came to Notre Dame wondering if I should have gone to the Air Force Academy instead. I was in freshman Air Force ROTC at Notre Dame, and

one day the cadets went down to Bunker Hill Air Force Base in Peru, Indiana, and I got face to face with a B-58 Hustler, a fighter-bomber, and realized that I was preparing to actually kill people, and I decided right there that Air Force ROTC was not for me. So, midway through my freshman year, my involvement with the ROTC program ended. That was just before I got a driver's license. In New York State, you had to wait until you were eighteen to drive.

TYDEMAN: *Yes.*

LOPEZ: I think because I had a driver's license there in my junior and senior years, the time I might have spent perfecting whatever skill I might have had as a soccer player, I spent trying to get out of town. Traveling to the Upper Peninsula in Michigan or driving to Mississippi or West Virginia, where I wrote about Odey Cassel's place, I just moved on from organized sports. Much in the same way, in my junior year, I fell out of the habit of daily Mass and Communion. There was no dramatic incident, no pivotal moment. I just ceased going to Mass and Communion every day. Something else began filling that place.

TYDEMAN: *So you never harbored any illusions about going on to professional sport?*

LOPEZ: No, I didn't have the skill, and I didn't have the ambition. Maybe if I had had the skill, I would have had the ambition, but I certainly didn't have the ambition. It was not a goal of mine to play professional ball. There wasn't enough of a life of the mind in it for me.

TYDEMAN: *And that was clear to you?*

LOPEZ: Yeah.

TYDEMAN: *You've mentioned an incident at Notre Dame that involved, you said, breaking away from your peer group, to the point that, I think you mentioned, you were spit on in public in the main quadrangle?*

LOPEZ: I have really puzzled over this, you know. A month or so ago, I got the Griffin Award from the university. It's given to a Notre Dame graduate who has achieved some measure of success as a writer. In preparing my remarks for accepting the award, I went back and looked through the four yearbooks of my undergraduate years at Notre Dame. I found so few points of identity on those pages, it was like I was reading the yearbooks of a school I'd never gone to. And it drove home for me the fact that I lived in my own world at Notre Dame. I took advantage of the courses that were offered, I worked at the radio station, I worked at the theater and studied hard and played soccer and was a good student, but I wasn't part of mainstream Notre Dame life. The reason I wasn't is because what Notre Dame represented—I'm saying this in hindsight—was not anything I could finally identify with. In my senior year, 1966, the issue of Vietnam was in the air. We were all aware as seniors that if we didn't go directly into graduate school we would likely be drafted. A group of us saw ourselves as conscientious objectors, or so we thought. We were Vietnam protestors, and we were also the kids who wore bell-bottom trousers and had long hair. So, the more conservative elements of this conservative school treated us with contempt and the kind of petty violence that characterizes mob behavior.

TYDEMAN: *To return to the world of freelance publishing, when you began publishing with North American Review and then later with Audubon, were those initial contacts you made? I mean did you follow the freelance model and send things in?*
LOPEZ: Yeah. I would go to New York and, on a very tight budget, see as many editors as I could, get as many assignments as I could from different magazines, and then go back to Oregon and try to write, to come through on all the assignments.

TYDEMAN: *One would imagine that you had to live pretty close to the bone during that time to make ends meet.*
LOPEZ: Yes, but I had some help from my family. My mother gave me a gasoline credit card, so my expenses for gas, for doing all that driving around the country, were covered.

TYDEMAN: *Another thing that isn't clear to me was your decision to give up graduate work at the University of Oregon and devote full time to writing. You've said you didn't see the fit. Could you elaborate?*

LOPEZ: By the time I finished a graduate degree at Notre Dame, in 1968, I had published a certain number of articles and stories but I didn't see how I could make my living as a writer. That meant the path for me as a writer was going to be teaching, and that meant getting an MFA, so I applied to several MFA programs and was accepted at Oregon. Oregon was a place I had visited when I was young, and it held out more geographical promise for me than programs in other parts of the country. So when I got accepted there I just went, on instinct. The University of Oregon had MFA programs in jewelry and metalsmithing, painting, dance, sculpture, ceramics, and theater—whatever happens, I thought, there's going to be a place for me there. I found the school academically inferior and the MFA program weak, and after that first semester I didn't know what to do. I had to salvage the expense of the move and make something of it, so I switched from liberal arts over to the School of Journalism, thinking I'd get an MS degree in journalism and maybe teach journalism as opposed to creative writing. But, like so many institutions, Oregon was an institution first, and what the degree program required of me was work I felt I had outgrown. All I really wanted to do was write. Barre Toelken advised me one day that the smartest thing I could do was to get out of there. He said, "You don't belong in graduate school, you should be writing." So with that push I left. I never finished the journalism degree. I think I was three or four courses shy of a second master's degree when I left. I worried about not finishing the degree, though, leaving the job undone. Four or five years later I went back and took a couple of courses, but I knew I was on to other things, that I had to let the degree go. It was a financial investment in tuition that didn't turn into a degree, and that bothered me, but I was happy doing what I was doing and committed to the new work. It was too late for me to go back to school.

TYDEMAN: *Right. How did you choose Oregon? I mean, you still were on the East Coast at that point?*
LOPEZ: Well, I was at Notre Dame, in Indiana. My younger brother and I had made a long trip through the West in the summer of 1964, and I'd worked on a ranch in Wyoming in 1965, I had my childhood experience in California, and my desire was to return to the West.

Whatever I was going to do, it felt like my life would unfold better there than back east. It wasn't a prejudiced decision, it was just the answer to a question: Where do you fit? My younger brother and I have talked about this a couple of times, and we've come to the conclusion—he's three years younger than I am, I was eleven and he was eight when we left California—that some emotional experiences important to young boys took place for me in the West and took place for him in the East. When he finished at Notre Dame, he moved back east, and that's where he's lived ever since. He lived for years on Block Island and then on Martha's Vineyard. He lives in Maine now, but he's toyed with the idea of living out here because our half-brother lives out here, in northern California. But I think he'll stay back east. That's just the place where he feels at ease. He understands the intelligence of that landscape.

TYDEMAN: *Another issue I wanted to bring up is the conscious decision not to write about friends or people you know. You allude to "The Toy Teacher," about your close friend Dick Showalter, as an "aha!" or key experience. From that time on, you made the decision that you wouldn't write about friends or people living in the area of Oregon you lived in. I understand how you might have developed a trust there that should never be compromised, but it also strikes me that that imposes a heavy burden on a writer. It seems to me that that landscape has shaped the form of your fiction.*

LOPEZ: I don't feel those issues of privacy as a burden. The structure of my short stories to begin with is, I guess, atypical. They do not adhere to the approved form, but I never felt any calling, as it happened, to write autobiographical fiction. I respect other people's privacy, and I like my own privacy to be respected. The form that I have arrived at for short fiction, in which characters are not based on people I know, and the landscape is rarely western Oregon, and little happens that is rooted in autobiography, suits me perfectly. Maybe what's missing for some in the way I approach fiction is just that, that I don't write autobiographically. I remember Robley Wilson saying something to me one time when I told him about a few events that occurred on St. Lawrence Island in the northern Bering Sea when I was there in 1981 writing a piece about hunting, incidents that weren't going to be mentioned in this long piece I was writing for him, "A Faint Light on the Northern Edge." He said, well that's okay, you know, you can always use them in a piece of fiction. I thought Robley would or might, but I wouldn't. Fiction for me always seemed to ask for a more extensive act of imagination. A story like "The Mappist" grows out of personal observation, of course. There's an incident in there where the narrator refers to being in the Sanseido bookstore in Jimbocho in Tokyo. Writing that scene, I'm recreating an evening I spent in that bookstore. But that's setting. With my characters, I have tried to steer clear of encroaching on someone else's personality or of including too much from my own life.

TYDEMAN: *That makes me think though, of course, of a question I was going to ask a little later on, about your life-long fascination with maps.*
LOPEZ: Yes. It was there from a very early age.

TYDEMAN: *Was it* National Geographic *initially or . . . ?*
LOPEZ: I can't remember when I first saw a copy of *National Geographic*, but my 1949 *Hammond's Illustrated Library World Atlas* was a transfixing book when I was seven, eight, nine years old. It played a big role in how I imagined myself. Maps, as you know, have been at the center of a lot of my work. There's a story, in fact, called "The Man Who Had Maps," which appeared in *North American Review* nearly twenty years before I wrote "The Mappist." It's a somewhat similar story.

TYDEMAN: *And you've also mentioned scrapbooking.*
LOPEZ: Yes. I asked a friend of mine, a therapist, whether, when you say something like "I've been thinking about this all of my life" even if you have no clear memory of those moments in which you are supposedly thinking about this thing, just an intuitive sense that you've been thinking about it for a long time, whether there is any way to verify you actually *have* been thinking about something for a long time. And he said if you have scrapbooks from an early age—five, six, seven, eight years old—those scrapbooks will reveal what you were paying attention to back then. At that age, you're responding

to things in an uncalculated way. You're responding viscerally to images the world offers, cutting these images out of magazines, because your enthusiasm for these symbols is genuine. He said if you still have scrapbooks from early in your life, you'll find in the imagery there the things that you're most deeply attached to. So, I went back to the scrapbooks I'd kept from childhood, and he was right. The images I cut out of magazines like *Life* and *Collier's* were about travel and geography and Native American settlements and life in the American West, about airplane flight and exploration. It might be interesting for somebody with the right frame of mind to just go through those two or three scrapbooks—they're probably only thirty pages each, it's not that much material—to see how much those images have to do with what came along in the way of books and stories during the next fifty years. I'd do it myself, but the idea of trying to define or summarize a life that is not yet over would make me skittish.

Afterword

ONE OF THE CONCEPTS MOST REVERED by Barry Lopez is expressed in the word *isumataq*, "storyteller," from the Inuktitut language of the eastern Canadian Arctic. He translates the word as "the person who creates the atmosphere in which wisdom reveals itself." Since the conclusion of these recorded conversations, Lopez has continued to write and tell stories, stories that contain a wisdom that benefits the community. Or as he put it in a recent interview, "The driving thing for me is if you are going to tell a story, tell a story that helps." An authentic story, in his view, ultimately is not about the writer but about us, the community. Over time his adherence to this position is absolute. He continues his work at Texas Tech University, but in recent years with an even greater emphasis on working with honors students from the Natural History–Humanities major (now called the Environment and Humanities Degree) that he and Edward O. Wilson designed. Since these interviews, Lopez—ever conscious of what he wants to do with the time he has left—has continued to create stories that matter.

He co-edited with Debra Gwartney one of the major recent works of cultural geography, *Home Ground*, first published in 2006. In 2011, the leading academic geographic organization in the United States, the Association of American Geographers, awarded him its prestigious prize of Honorary Geographer. It is given each year to an individual "as a way of recognizing excellence in research, teaching, or writing on geographic topics by non-geographers." Past award members include Paul Krugman, John McPhee, and Stephen J. Gould. His shorter work has appeared in *The Georgia Review, Harper's, Orion, Portland*

Magazine, and *TriQuarterly.* His work with Frank Stewart produced two issues of the journal *Manoa* devoted to the theme of reconciliation. He has continued to speak and deliver lectures and readings around the country and overseas, where he shares his vision and invites his audience to think about, or engage in conversations with him about, the meaning of justice.

At these public events Lopez is at pains to emphasize that although he is, above all else, a writer, his work does have an activist component. This is a key to understanding all of his work. For the two issues of *Manoa* on reconciliation, co-edited with Stewart, he sought out the perspectives of other writers from South America, Europe, and Africa. His work with Archbishop Desmond Tutu had a similar motivation— a writer seeking ways to convey to his readers the complexity and larger international implications of various forms of reconciliation. More recently, in collaboration with Alan Magee and other artists and writers, he has been working to create a broader awareness of the inutility of war.

In the years since I recorded these conversations, he has continued to travel the world visiting some of the most ravaged landscapes on earth—southern Lebanon and Afghanistan, northern Sumatra after the Boxing Day Tsunami, the iron ore mining country of Western Australia—and some of its more haunted and inspiring places—the Paleolithic cave at Altamira, the majestic fjords of western Greenland, American Indian battlefields, and the concentration camps at Auschwitz and Birkenau. In 2010 Bill Moyers, who had invited Lopez to be his guest on the final airing of the award-winning PBS television series *Bill Moyers Journal,* said, "I thought long and hard about who I would invite to be the last guest on the *Journal.* So many people have inspired my own work that I had a difficult time making a choice. But I finally decided to ask someone whose curiosity about the world, and the pursuit of it, have set the gold standard for all of us whose work it is to explain those things we don't understand."

The essay "Sliver of Sky," which appeared in the January 2013 issue of *Harper's* and which addresses the sexual abuse Lopez endured as a young boy, demonstrates how a writer, by carefully structuring his ideas and using a moderate tone, can open the doors on a volatile issue that threatens the social fabric of an entire culture. For Lopez, writing in depth about the abuse was not an act of personal catharsis; rather, it was a writer's effort to frame effectively a widespread and horrific problem.

As this book goes to press, Lopez is about to embark on a long journey that will eventually take him to Peru, Cambodia, Tanzania, and Morocco. Fueled by a desire to encounter other cultures on their own ground in a time of international tension and disruptive globalization, this trip will also mark the final stage of research for his forthcoming book. As he prepared for this departure, I was reminded by Debra Gwartney, his wife and the author of the powerful memoir *Live Through This*, of something her husband said in a keynote address at the presentation of the 2008 Whiting Award for emerging writers, at the Pierpont Morgan Library. These words invite us again to walk the hallowed path of the imagination and typify Lopez's high ideals: "Be tireless and devoted to the courtship of your imagination. Nurture your friendships, your allegiance with other human beings. If you feel grief, or rage, or love, give it a shape so we readers will know what you mean, and be able to better understand, better cope with the land-scapes of our grief, and rage, and love."

Works by Barry Lopez

Compiled by Diane Warner

BARRY LOPEZ'S PROFESSIONAL CAREER as a magazine writer began in 1966, when he started writing for several Catholic magazines on the political left (*Ave Maria, a.d.*) and for a couple of automotive magazines (*Popular Imported Cars, Autodriver*) published by his stepfather. By the late sixties and early seventies he was writing largely for environmental publications (*National Wildlife, Not Man Apart, Pacific Wilderness Journal, Audubon, Environmental Action*) and, then and later, for general-interest publications (*Travel & Leisure, Harper's, Popular Science, Outside, Popular Mechanics*), focusing on a variety of subjects, including travel, the practical use of tools and machinery, natural history, and outdoor life. In 1971 he became an early contributor to the *Washington Post's* Style section, and between 1970 and 1973 he wrote a number of articles for *Northwest*, the Sunday magazine of the (Portland) *Oregonian*. His essays, short stories, and interviews began appearing in literary journals (*Skywriting, Tales, Chouteau Review, Contemporary Literature in Translation, Dalmo'ma*) in 1972. By 1976, the year his first book, *Desert Notes*, was published, his short fiction and essays were beginning to appear regularly in *North American Review* and *Harper's*, where he would begin long periods of work with, respectively, Robley Wilson and Lewis Lapham. Since then, his essays and stories have appeared regularly in a wide range of periodicals, and his publishing life has become more complex.

This bibliography is intended to aid researchers in identifying and locating all written work in English by Barry Lopez. In addition to his many books, the bibliography includes the first North American publication of his essays, short stories, book reviews, introductions, fine press editions, and broadsides. In the contents lists supplied for volumes of collected works, date of first publication is stated for items previously published, for example "Buffalo" (1976) in the list for *Winter Count*, or "Landscape and Narrative" (1984) in the list for *Crossing Open Ground*. The text of a short story or essay collected in a book by Lopez is the definitive text. The bibliography also notes when a piece has been selected for inclusion in a special annual anthology or collection such as *The Best American Essays* series or "best" writing from *The Georgia Review* or *National Geographic*. Annotations have been provided to set particularly important or significant pieces in context and to provide the researcher with background information or unique insight into a piece. As an aid to researchers, it should be noted that Barry Lopez was born Barry Holstun Brennan. He became Barry Holstun Lopez in 1956 when he was adopted by Adrian Lopez. He published occasionally under the name Barry Holstun Lopez until the late seventies and only as Barry Lopez thereafter.

Formal introductions Lopez has written for various books are listed in the section "Forewords, Introductions, and Catalog and Calendar Essays." Other pieces in the author's oeuvre, also entitled "Introduction," deserve some explanation. According to the author, the first piece in *Desert Notes*, called "Introduction" and written at the publisher's request, was meant to be a nonfiction introduction to a collection of fictional pieces. The first piece in *River Notes*, also called "Introduction," and the first piece in *Field Notes*, called "Introduction: Within Birds' Hearing," are works of fiction but were given these titles to keep the contents of these two books parallel with the contents of the first book in that loose-knit trilogy.

Books

Desert Notes: Reflections in the Eye of a Raven. Kansas City, MO: Sheed, Andrews & McMeel, 1976. Contents: "Introduction," "Desert Notes" (1973), "The Hot Spring," "The Raven," "Twilight" (1976), "Perimeter," "The Blue Mound People," "Conversation," "The School," "The Wind," "Coyote and Rattlesnake" (1976), "Directions."

Giving Birth to Thunder, Sleeping with His Daughter: Coyote Builds North America. Kansas City, KS: Sheed Andrews and McMeel, 1978. [Thirteen of the sixty-eight stories in this collection previously appeared in *Chouteau Review* (1975), *McKenzie Enterprise* (1976), *Dalmo'ma* (1978), and *Skywriting* (1978).]

Of Wolves and Men. New York: Charles Scribner's Sons, 1978.

River Notes: The Dance of Herons. Kansas City, MO: Andrews and McMeel, 1979. Contents: "Introduction," "The Search for the Heron," "The Log Jam," "The Bend," "The Falls," "The Shallows," "The Rapids," "The Salmon," "Hanner's Story," "Dawn," "Upriver," "Drought."

Winter Count. New York: Charles Scribner's Sons, 1981. Contents: "Restoration," "Winter Herons," "Buffalo" (1976), "The Orrery," "Winter Count" (1973), "Geese, They Flew Over in a Storm," "The Tapestry," "The Woman Who Had Shells," "The Lover of Words" (1980), "The Location of the River."

Arctic Dreams: Imagination and Desire in a Northern Landscape. New York: Charles Scribner's Sons, 1986.

Crossing Open Ground. New York: Charles Scribner's Sons, 1988. Contents: "The Stone Horse" (1986), "A Reflection on White Geese" (1982), "Gone Back into the Earth" (1981), "Trying the Land" (1979), "Landscape and Narrative" (1984), "Yukon-Charley, The Shape of Wilderness" (1982), "Borders" (1981), "The Bull Rider" (1978), "A Presentation of Whales" (1980), "Children in the Woods" (1982), "The Lives of Seals" (1982), "Searching for Ancestors" (1983), "Grown Men" (1979), "The Passing Wisdom of Birds" (1985).

Crow and Weasel. Illustrations by Tom Pohrt. San Francisco: North Point Press, 1990.

The Rediscovery of North America. Lexington: University Press of Kentucky, 1991. [The inaugural Thomas D. Clark Lecture at the University of Kentucky.]

Field Notes: The Grace Note of the Canyon Wren. New York: Alfred A. Knopf, 1994. Contents: "Introduction: Within Birds' Hearing," "Teal Creek," "Empira's Tapestry," "The Open Lot," "Conversation," "Pearyland" (1994), "The Negro in the Kitchen," "The Entreaty of the Wiideema" (1994), "Homecoming," "Sonora," "Lessons from the Wolverine," "The Runner."

Lessons from the Wolverine. Illustrations by Tom Pohrt. Athens: University of Georgia Press, 1997.

About This Life: Journeys on the Threshold of Memory. New York: Alfred A.
Knopf, 1998. Contents: "A Voice" (1998), "Searching for Depth in
Bonaire" (1996), "A Short Passage in Northern Hokkaido" (1986),
"Orchids on the Volcanoes" (1989), "Informed by Indifference" (1988),
"Flight" (1995), "Apologia" (1989), "In a Country of Light, among
Animals" (1981), "The American Geographies" (1989), "Effleurage: The
Stroke of Fire" (1998), "The Whaleboat" (1998), "Replacing Memory"
(1993), "A Passage of the Hands" (1997), "Learning to See" (1998),
"Death," "Murder" (1981, 1998), "Speed," "Theft."

Apologia. Woodcuts by Robin Eschner. Athens: University of Georgia Press, 1998.

Light Action in the Caribbean. New York: Alfred A. Knopf, 2000. Contents:
"Remembering Orchards" (1991), "Stolen Horses" (2000), "Thomas
Lowdermilk's Generosity" (1993), "In the Garden of the Lords of War"
(1996), "Emory Bear Hands' Birds" (1999), "In the Great Bend of the
Souris River" (1997), "The Deaf Girl" (1999), "Rubén Mendoza Vega,
Suzuki Professor of Early Caribbean History, University of Florida at
Gainesville, Offers a History of the United States Based on Personal
Experience" (1994), "The Letters of Heaven" (1997), "Mornings in
Quarain" (1996), "The Construction of the *Rachel*," "Light Action in the
Caribbean," "The Mappist" (2000).

Of Wolves and Men. New York: Charles Scribner's Sons, 2004. With new
afterword and expanded bibliography.

Vintage Lopez. New York: Vintage Books, 2004. Contents: "Landscape and
Narrative," from *Crossing Open Ground;* "Learning to See," from *About
This Life;* "Flight," from *About This Life;* "The American Geographies,"
from *About This Life;* "Prologue, Pond's Bay, Baffin Island," from *Arctic
Dreams;* "The Naturalist"; "The Entreaty of the Wiideema," from *Field
Notes;* "Teal Creek," from *Field Notes;* "The Woman Who Had Shells,"
from *Winter Count;* "The Letters of Heaven," from *Light Action in the
Caribbean;* "Restoration," from *Winter Count;* "The Mappist," from *Light
Action in the Caribbean.*

Resistance. New York: Alfred A. Knopf, 2004. Contents: "Apocalypse," "Río
de la Plata," "Mortise and Tenon," "Traveling to Bo Ling," "The Bear in
the Road," "The Walls of Yogpar," "Laguna de Bay in A-Sharp," "Nílch'i,"
"Flight from Berlin."

Home Ground: Language for an American Landscape. Edited by Barry Lopez
and Debra Gwartney, with an introduction by Barry Lopez. San Antonio,
TX: Trinity University Press, 2006. Including Lopez's definitions for

blind creek (36), desert (102), ice volcano (188), mudslide (239), pitch (270), refugium (293), sand (311), scarp (316), shinnery (325), soil (335), and strike valley (345).

Fine Press Editions

Desert Reservation. Port Townsend, WA: Copper Canyon Press, 1980. Published in an edition of 300 in paper wraps, 26 of which are signed and lettered. Designed and printed by Tree Swenson and David Romtvedt.

Coyote Love: Native American Folktales. Portland, ME: Coyote Love Press, 1989. Published in an edition of 99. Three Trickster stories, adapted by Lopez from *Giving Birth to Thunder:* "Coyote and Beaver Exchange Wives," "Coyote Marries His Daughter," and "Coyote Visits the Women." Illustrations by Gary Buch. Hand-illuminated by Allen Wong. Printed on Dresden Ingres paper, using Goudy Thirty, Kennerly, and Neuland types, and bound in Mexican bark covers, all by George Bennington.

Children in the Woods. Eugene, OR: lone goose press, 1992. Published in an edition of 75, numbered and signed by the artist, Margaret Prentice, and Lopez. Essay from *Crossing Open Ground.* Woodcut illustrations, handmade abaca cover and text papers by Margaret Prentice. Typeset and bound by Sandy Tilcock and Kathleen Wigley. Designed and boxed by Sandy Tilcock.

Looking in a Deeper Lair. Eugene, OR: lone goose press, 1996. Published in an edition of 179 (150 numbered, signed, soft-cover copies and 29 deluxe, hardcover copies, signed and boxed; of the deluxe edition 26 are lettered A through Z and 3 are designated artist's copies). Eulogy for Wallace Stegner, with an intaglio print by Suellen Larkin. Designed, printed, and bound by Sandy Tilcock.

Apologia. Eugene, OR: lone goose press, 1997. Published in an edition of 50 (16 copies reserved for the participants). With 23 woodcuts by Robin Eschner, designed to form a single continuous image. Designed by Charles Hobson. Edition printer, Nora Pauwels; letterpress printer, Susan Acker; binder, John DeMeritt. Boxed by Sandy Tilcock. Tire-tread print on Wyoming topographic map created by Barry Lopez and Sandy Tilcock and included in book pocket. Accordion bound.

The Letters of Heaven. Eugene, OR: Knight Library Press, 2000. Published in an edition of 125 numbered copies, signed by the artist and author. Short story from *Light Action in the Caribbean,* with five hand-colored etchings by Robin Eschner. Calligraphic title, headings, and ornaments by Marilyn Reaves. Designed, printed, and bound by Sandy Tilcock.

Anotaciones. San Francisco: Pacific Editions, 2001. Published in an edition of 30. Story entitled "Ruben Mendoza Vega . . ." from *Light Action in the Caribbean.* Accordion-bound book with sixteen footnotes printed on laser-cut puzzle pieces, all contained in an actual cigar box, enclosed with chemise. Assembling the puzzle organizes the footnotes. Book designed by Charles Hobson. Inkjet monotype, color photography, and offset lithography. Foldout reference sheet.

Pulling Wire. Northfield, MN: Red Dragonfly Press, 2004. Published in an edition of 225. Title page woodcut by Gary Young. Designed and printed by Scott King.

Barry Lopez. Eugene, OR: lone goose press, 2005. Published in an edition of 150 for attendees at a fundraising dinner for BRING, a recycling nonprofit organization in Eugene, March 31, 2005, at which Lopez spoke. Text is three paragraphs from "Apocalypse" in *Resistance*, pp. 17–18. Designed, printed, and bound by Sandy Tilcock.

The Mappist. San Francisco: Pacific Editions, 2005. Published in an edition of 48, numbered and signed. Nine monotypes with pastel by Charles Hobson printed as digital pigment images, and three reproductions with commentary from "The Topographic Maps of the United States" by the Director, United States Geological Survey, November 1937. Bound in boards wrapped with a reproduction of a 1911 map of Bogotá. Concertina binding uses original USGS maps. Letterpress printed in a Garamond Narrow typeface on BFK Rives paper by Les Ferriss. Interior slipcase and covers made by John DeMerritt with Kris Langan. Designed by Charles Hobson with Alice Shaw.

The Near Woods. Berkeley, CA: Tangram Press, 2005. Published in an edition of 165. With two monotypes with pastel by Charles Hobson, reproduced with digital pigment prints and tipped in. Designed, printed, and sewn by Jerry Reddan.

The Near Woods. San Francisco: Pacific Editions, 2006. Edition of 26 lettered copies. Using pages from the Tangram Press edition of 2005. Bound in boards by Charles Hobson with the assistance of Alice Shaw and covered with a reproduction of "Dosino del Rancho San Miguelito," ca. 1841, a drawing used to establish land grants in California. Includes a hand-colored digital pigment print by Charles Hobson as a back folder.

¡Nunca Mas! Northfield, MN: Red Dragonfly Press, 2007. Published in an edition of 350 copies, 90 of which are numbered and signed by the author and artist. Wood engraving, "Gate of Death" [Birkenau], by Carol Inderieden. Designed, printed offset, and sewn by Scott King.

Outside. Santa Rosa, CA: Nawakum Press, 2013. Six stories, two each from *Desert Notes, River Notes,* and *Field Notes,* with 11 engravings by Barry Moser. Published in an edition of 50: 28 Roman-numeraled slipcased volumes; 12 lettered, deluxe boxed volumes; and 10 numbered volumes reserved for the press and participants. Each volume signed by the author and the artist. Designed by Barry Moser. Introduction by James Perrin Warren. Afterword by the author. Printed by Arthur Larson, Horton Tank Graphics, Hadley, MA. Binding, boxes, and slipcases by Craig Jensen, BookLab II, San Marcos, TX. Marbled paper by Pam Smith, Abiquiu, NM. Calligraphy by Judythe Seick, Santa Fe, NM. Published at Nawakum Press by David Pascoe.

Journal, Magazine, and Newspaper Publications

1966

"The Sun Was Gone." *Man to Man,* January 1966, 20–21, 54–56, 62.

"Spider." *Man to Man,* March 1966, 20–21, 61–62.

"The Gift." *Ave Maria,* March 19, 1966, 22–23.

> When Lopez was a senior at Notre Dame, his roommate, an editor at *Ave Maria,* took this story off Lopez's desk and showed it to managing editor Jim Andrews, who liked it and published it. Ten years later, Andrews would publish Lopez's first book, *Desert Notes.* This story marks the beginning of Lopez's professional relationship with a group of people at *Ave Maria* who in 1970 would establish *a.d.* magazine and then go on to work at the *Washington Post.*

1967

Unsigned editorial material. *Sir!,* July 1967.

"Morocco." *Sir!,* September 1967, 4–6, 73.

Unsigned editorial material. *Man to Man,* November 1967.

"The Psychedelic Christ." *Notre Dame Dialog,* December 1967, 24–25.

1968

"Beneath." *Ave Maria,* March 2, 1968, 28–29.

"The Crucifixion of Christ." *Ave Maria,* March 23, 1968, 11–15. Photographs by Justin Soleta.

> The first of five pieces Lopez wrote to accompany photo essays by Soleta for *Ave Maria,* where Soleta was on the staff, and for other magazines, including *U.S. Catholic* and *Our Family.*

"Hillclimbing, An Afternoon at a Little League Hill." *Mr.,* April 1968, 38–41, 61–62.

> First publication of a type of story Lopez would go on to write regularly. Here, he looked past the negative middle-class response to motorcycle hill-climbing in order to explore elements of risk and self-respect. A similar story, "Going Down with the Bulls," would appear in *North American Review* in 1974.

"Until Death Do Us Part." *Ave Maria,* June 29, 1968, 26–28.

"The Other Side of Police Brutality." *Focus Michiana,* July 1968, 16–17.

> In the summer of 1968, Lopez and John Twohey founded *Focus Michiana,* a city magazine published in South Bend, Indiana. Police brutality in the city was a controversial topic, and Lopez wanted to address the policemen's side of the argument. He wrote stories for the magazine's first three issues before leaving for Oregon and turning management of the magazine over to Twohey.

"Drugs in Our High Schools." *Focus Michiana,* August 1968, 12–15.

Unsigned editorial material. *Focus Michiana,* September 1968.

1969

"Miniature Museum for Big Wagons." *Real West,* April 1969, 40–43.

> First publication of an article that brings together elements that will surface repeatedly in Lopez's later fiction. Here he wrote about an older man, Ivan Collins, a painstaking and disciplined craftsman with no university degree, who built miniature, one-of-a-kind, horse-drawn wagons for display in a small basement room the University of Oregon provided for him.

"Odey's." *Ave Maria,* June 7, 1969, 16–19.

> An early attempt to address the relationship between an older man, Odey Cassel, and a younger man, the author. Ten years later Lopez wrote "Grown Men" for *Notre Dame Magazine,* a fuller exploration of his history with Odey Cassel and two other older men. This mentor/apprentice imagery would come to the fore in many of his later short stories, including, for example, "The Orrery" in *Winter Count* and "Remembering Orchards" in *Light Action in the Caribbean.*

"Toyota Land Cruiser." *Autodriver,* August 1969, 6–11, 62. [Not the same as the article that appears in the September 1973 issue of *Popular Imported Cars.*]

"'Junk' Will Make Any House Your Home." *Lady's Circle,* September 1969, 36–37, 72–73.

"Outward Bound." *Strobe,* September 1969, 46–49, 68–69.

> Northwest Outward Bound was the flagship school of the British Outward Bound movement in the United States. Several of its instructors were Lopez's friends, and he agreed with much of the philosophy behind this teaching. Outward Bound was also an important incubator at this time for environmental activism in the Pacific Northwest.

"Ford's Bronco, The Mountain Mustang." *Autodriver,* October 1969, 4–7, 61–62.

"Nessie the USO." *Man to Man,* October 1969, 6–7, 55–56.

"Gull in the Rocks." *Ave Maria,* October 25, 1969, 13–14.

> Essay about Lopez's encounter with a seagull on the Oregon coast. The dying bird had apparently been poisoned. The story is an early example of his concern for the lives of animals, the state of the environment, and ethical human behavior.

"Getting into *Getting Straight.*" *Strobe,* November 1969, 64–68.

"Land-Rover, 88 Inches of Get There!" *Popular Imported Cars,* November 1969, 6–7, 55. [Not the same as the article that appears in the December 1969 issue of *Autodriver.*]

"Ecological Rape." *Oregon Daily Emerald,* November 18, 1969, 5.

"People, A Town in Defense of Itself." *Ave Maria,* November 29, 1969, 23–27.

> In the winter of 1969 a storm dumped three feet of snow on Eugene, Oregon, in a thirty-six-hour period. Lopez wrote about the range of people's responses to this natural event.

"Land-Rover, 88 Inches of Get There!" *Autodriver,* December 1969, 4–7, 62. [Not the same as the article that appears in the November 1969 issue of *Popular Imported Cars.*]

"The Garage Theory, A Metaphysical Game." *Ave Maria,* December 6, 1969, 6–7.

> Lopez published several essays like this in the late sixties and early seventies in which he philosophized about human social organization.

1970

"Four-Wheel Drive Kaiser Jeep." *Autodriver,* February 1970, 4–7, 60–61.

"Jean's, the First Time Around." *a.d.,* March 28, 1970, 18–19.

Ave Maria, to which Lopez contributed frequently, was replaced by *a.d.,* a magazine with an ecumenical spirit that celebrated social activism and ethical responsibility. He wrote three pieces for a column called "Flavor of the Seventies," of which this was the first, in the first issue. When the magazine folded a year after it was established, one of its editors, Joel Garreau, went to the Style section of the *Washington Post,* and Lopez began writing occasionally for that section of the paper.

"International Harvester Scout." *Autodriver,* April 1970, 16–19, 56–57.

Unsigned editorial material. *a.d.,* April 5–11, 1970, 8.

"Toyota Corolla." *Popular Imported Cars,* May 1970, 4–7.

"The Widening Gyre." *a.d.,* May 3–9, 1970, 18–19.

"Let's Clear the Air." *Oregonian* [Portland], Northwest Magazine section, June 7, 1970, 15.

The first of nine pieces Lopez wrote for the paper's Sunday magazine.

"An Animal's Ability . . ." *a.d.,* June 14, 1970, 18–19.

"Chevy's Blazer." *Autodriver,* August 1970, 8–11, 53–54.

"Recreational Vehicle Boom." *Toyota Today,* Fall 1970, 20.

"The Piggy Back Bug." *Popular Imported Cars,* September 1970, 36–37.

"Which Four-Wheel Drive for You?" *Autodriver,* October 1970, 4–7, 53.

"Trueviews, Movies." *True,* October 1970, 22.

Lopez interviewed the actor Paul Newman in Newport, Oregon, on the set of *Sometimes a Great Notion,* a film based on the novel by Oregon writer Ken Kesey, and wrote this unsigned report.

1971

"Electric Trucking." *Bullfrog Information Service* 1.6 (1971), 24–25, 30.

"Datsun 1200 Coupe." *Popular Imported Cars,* January 1971, 34–37.

"Toyota Land Cruiser Station Wagon." *Popular Imported Cars,* January 1971, 24–27, 62.

"Show Me to the Student's Library." *Old Oregon,* January–February 1971, 14–16.

"A Place of Refuge." *Cascades,* February 1971, 26–29.

"Remember Man." *The Parent Educator,* February 1971, 12–13.

Lopez wrote this fictional piece for *Remember Man* (Ave Maria Press, 1971), compiled and edited by Charles Jones. It appears here for the first time, with Jones listed as the author and the title of the book substituted for Lopez's title, "Meditation."

"Toyota Wrapup." *Popular Imported Cars,* March 1971, 34–37.

"What You Need to Know Before You Buy a Four-Wheel Drive." *Popular Science,* March 1971, 76–77, 137.

One of a number of articles Lopez wrote during this time for this and similar publications, such as *Popular Mechanics,* about the practical use of motor vehicles and outdoor equipment.

"A New Sea." *International Surfing,* March 1971, 62–64.

"Toyota Corolla in '71." *Popular Imported Cars,* March 1971, 24–25, 59–60.

"County in Oregon Cleans Up Its Air." *New York Times,* March 7, 1971, no page, no section.

"To Begin With . . ." *Register-Guard* [Eugene, OR], Emerald Empire Magazine section, March 14, 1971, 6.

"Roscoe's Story, Going Underground in America." *Washington Post,* April 26, 1971, B1–B2.

Lopez reports on a man arrested by the FBI for avoiding the military draft. "This article marks a turning point for me because of its political content and the venue for its publication, the front page of the paper's Style section."

"Up Against the Ecological Wall." *Way,* May 1971, 16–18.

Lopez had a short relationship with this magazine, published in San Francisco. Like *a.d.* (see above), *Way* was interested in publishing reflections on ethical behavior and the spiritual dimensions of everyday life. This piece was about the ethical complexity presented by some environmental problems.

"Paradental Education, a New Look." *Cal,* June 1971, 20–22.

"Whole Earth's Suicide Party." *Washington Post,* June 14, 1971, B1, B6.

"I attended a party celebrating publication of the last issue of the *Whole Earth Catalog,* having promised editor Joel Garreau I would produce a story for the following day's edition of the paper. When the party continued well past midnight, I asked Garreau to be released from the assignment because of the unanticipated complexity of the event, hosted by Stewart Brand. Garreau insisted I meet the deadline. I did, but told Garreau this would be my last piece of hard-news reporting. I felt such deadlines left too little room to reflect on the meaning of such culturally significant events."

"'The Box' and How to Live with It." *Oregonian* [Portland], Northwest Magazine section, June 27, 1971, 10–11.

"The Environment and Your Toyota." *Toyota Topics,* Summer 1971, 24–25.

"Perfecting the Four-Wheel Drive." *Popular Imported Cars,* July 1971, 12–15.

"A New Wheel with Built-In Suspension." *Popular Imported Cars,* July 1971, 32–33, 58–59.

"Controversy over Anacapa—The Island Time Left Behind." *Washington Post.* July 22, 1971, C1–C2.

One of three pieces Lopez wrote about California's Channel Islands after he became interested in the movement to establish a national park there. His photographs that accompanied the story documented controversial behavior by National Park Service employees. Together with the story, they raised the national profile of this local environmental issue.

"*African Queen* at Work in Wilds of Oregon." *New York Times,* August 15, 1971, 64.

An environmentally sensitive developer in central Oregon purchased this famous boat, built for the movie of the same name, and used it to ferry guests at his Deschutes River resort. Lopez worked briefly as a stringer for the *New York Times* before the paper began to object to the number of pieces he was contributing to the *Washington Post.*

"How to Clean Up the Environment and Save Yourself Money." *Lady's Circle,* September 1971, 24–25, 57.

"A Walk in the Woods." *Outdoor World,* September–October 1971, 8–15.

"Weaving Made Simple." *Lady's Circle,* October 1971, 32–33.

"They Said This Was Supposed to Be Some Sort of Survival Thing." *Oregonian* [Portland], Northwest Magazine section, November 14, 1971, 8–11.

"On the Brink of a Park." *Not Man Apart,* December 1971, 16–19.

Lopez says he appreciated the encouragement of Tom Turner, editor of this front-line environmental publication, who allowed him to explore some of the biases that characterized environmentalists' zealous determination to establish a national park in California's Channel Islands.

1972

"Interview, Charles Simic." *Skywriting* 1.2 (1972), 24–31.

One of only two interviews Lopez has conducted and published. See "He Came to Talk" (1972) for a related story based on this interview and a public reading by Simic. See "The Leadership Imperative . . ." (2007) for the other interview.

"Small Cars Ain't So Small." *Popular Imported Cars,* January 1972, 46–49.

Lopez wrote several pieces around this time that celebrated the fuel economy and superior workmanship of foreign cars.

"Survival Experience." *College and University Journal,* January 1972, 30–32.

"Toyota Celica ST." *Popular Imported Cars,* January 1972, 4–7, 60.

"The Dam Broke." *Register-Guard* [Eugene, OR], January 22, 1972, 4A.

"Channel Islands Controversy." *Not Man Apart,* 2.4 (April 1972), 16.

>Response to letters written in reaction to "On the Brink of a Park" in *Not Man Apart,* December 1971.

"Emphasis on Craftsmanship." *Register-Guard* [Eugene, OR], April 22, 1972, C1–2.

"Getting Away from It All." *Toyota Topics,* Spring 1972, 23–27.

"The *Queen* Steams Again." *Toyota Topics,* Spring 1972, 6–7.

"Audi 100LS." *Popular Imported Cars,* July 1972, 8–11, 61–62.

"He Came to Talk." *Oregonian* [Portland], Northwest Magazine section, July 2, 1972, 12–13.

>An article about poet Charles Simic See "Interview, Charles Simic" (1972).

"The Toy Teacher." *Oregonian* [Portland], Northwest Magazine section, July 23, 1972, 4–7.

>Lopez's first effort to write about a close friend, wood worker and toy maker Richard Showalter. Although Showalter agreed to be interviewed and photographed, the experience led Lopez to decide he would not write again about either his friends or the area in Oregon where he lived. He wrote about Showalter again, however, in "Trying the Land" in *Harper's* (February 1979), and *River Notes* (1979) is clearly set in the McKenzie River valley, where Lopez continues to live.

"Camping without a Fire—Yes." *Oregonian* [Portland], Northwest Magazine section, July 23, 1972, 7.

"Getting Away from the Great Getaway." *Oregonian* [Portland], Northwest Magazine section, August 13, 1972.

"It's Not Easy to Love a Deformed Child." *U.S. Catholic,* September 1972, 24–30. Photographs by Justin Soleta.

"The Nez Perce Country." *Oregonian* [Portland], Northwest Magazine section, September 10, 1972, 12–13.

"The Earth's Great Cycles." *Earthlight,* October 9, 1972, 1–2.

>When Josh Gitomer, an editor at *Not Man Apart,* founded this environmental publication for children, Lopez offered to write a series on the cycling of nitrogen and other elements in the Earth's ecosystems.

"Error Message." *College and University Journal,* November 1972, 25–28.

"Journey to a Secret Place." *Outdoor World,* November–December 1972, 10–16.

"What You Don't Know about Marijuana." *Sir!,* December 1972, 26–27, 80–82.

1973

"The Child in the Shadow of the Tree." *U.S. Catholic,* February 1973, 22–28. Photographs by Justin Soleta.

"In Little Things I Find the Cosmos." *National Wildlife,* February–March 1973, 42–47.

"In Praise of the Circle." *Environmental Action,* March 31, 1973, 8–11.

"The Chinese Cure." *Sir!,* April 1973, 34–36, 86–88.

"Datsun 240Z." *Popular Imported Cars,* May 1973, 4–7.

"The Empty Promise of Freedom." *Environmental Action,* May 26, 1973, 9–11.

"Weekend." *Audubon,* July 1973, 62–67.

> Lopez's first large-scale essay on an environmental theme. He spent a weekend in the central Oregon desert, a trip that ended at Lake Billy Chinook, a reservoir. This essay conveys bewilderment and contempt as he confronts the highly mechanized activities of American families on vacation.

"Translation—The Indian's Dilemma." *The Oregonian* [Portland], Northwest Magazine section, July 29, 1973, 12–15.

> Lopez reflects here for the first time on what will become a major theme in his work: the wisdom of Native American traditions and the general failure of American society to recognize or give credence to these ideas.

"Fall." *Toyota Topics,* Fall 1973, 4–5.

"Desert Notes." *Skywriting* 1.3 (September 1973), no pagination.

> This short fiction piece was the foundation for Lopez's first book, *Desert Notes.*

"How to Raise Your Kids in a Pick-Up Truck." *U.S. Catholic,* September 1973, 26–31. Photographs by Justin Soleta.

"As Oregon Goes, So the Nation?" *Environmental Action,* December 22, 1973, 7–10.

1974

"Land Rover." *Popular Imported Cars,* January 1974, 22–25, 52.

"Worlds of Country Inn Cookery: The New." *Washington Post,* January 24, 1974, E1, E7.

"Winter Four-Wheeling." *Saga,* March 1974, 24–25, 39, 44–45, 53.

"American Sketchbook: Notes in Common." *Notre Dame Magazine,* April 1974, 16–31.

> Lopez's first piece for his alma mater's alumni magazine.

"New Power Winches Wind Up Your Work Quicker." *Popular Science,* April 1974, 108–10, 160.

"Practice Session." *McKenzie Enterprise* 1.1 (April 25–May 8, 1974), 5. Photo essay.

"Faces of Where We Have Been." *North American Review,* Spring 1974, 3–7.
    Together, this essay and the one above in *Notre Dame Magazine* comprise Lopez's first major travel piece. "In December 1973, I drove from my home in Oregon to the Florida Everglades and back. I visited the Teapot Dome in Wyoming and other sites important in America's industrial history and was in the press pool for the launch of Apollo 17. The essay was too long for Robley Wilson at *North American Review,* where I first submitted it. When an editor at *Notre Dame Magazine* learned of the manuscript, he arranged with Wilson to publish one part of the essay while Wilson published the other part."

"Sacred Mountain." *Outdoor World,* Spring 1974, 24–25.

"Going Down with the Bulls." *North American Review.* Summer 1974, 3–7.
    Lopez attended various rodeos in 1973, including the Pendleton Roundup and the National Finals Rodeo in Oklahoma City. He was particularly drawn to the character and performance of several bull riders. By this time, *North American Review* had become the principal venue for his nonfiction.

"The Pendleton Round-up." *Toyota Topics,* Summer 1974, 14–17.

"Smaller Campfires." *Pacific Wilderness Journal,* June–July 1974, 28–29.

"Destruction on Wheels Out Where the Road Ends." *Environmental Action,* August 17, 1974, 4–6.

"Falling at Wagon Wheel Pass." *McKenzie Enterprise,* August 16–31, 1974, 6–7. Photo essay.

"Bad Shoes." *Harpoon,* September 1974, 28–31.
    Lopez wrote several pieces for this humor magazine, edited by his brother, Dennis Lopez.

"Walk the Roads." *Harpoon,* September 1974, 22–25.

"Being Born at Home Is Wonderful." *Lady's Circle,* October 1974, 26–27, 58–59.

"For Climbers, a Locking Sling Step." *Popular Science,* October 1974, 165.

"Learn from the Pros How to Fell a Tree." *Popular Science,* November 1974, 112–13, 137.

Unsigned editorial material. *Harpoon,* November 1974, various pages.

"Of the Mountains before There Were Names." *Contemporary Literature in Translation,* Fall–Winter 1974, 5–7.
    In coursework with one of his most important mentors, Barre Toelken at the University of Oregon, an expert on Native American culture, Lopez

had begun reworking scholarly renderings of Native American stories, especially Trickster tales, looking for a less formal and more respectful way of retelling them. This is one of several stories to come out of that work.

"How to Cut Free Firewood in the National Forests." *Popular Science,* December 1974, 93–95.

"Reflections on a Waiting Dog." *Lady's Circle,* December 1974, 44, 70–71.

"I was driving through Fort Benton, Montana, when I realized that the train station here was the place where the dog Shep, an American folk icon, had waited faithfully for six years for his deceased master to return. My affection for dogs and my tendency to see virtue in their behavior compelled this brief travel piece."

"Oregon's Big Trees." *Oregonian* [Portland], Northwest Magazine section, December 8, 1974, 6–7.

1975

"New Power Winches for RV's." *Motorcamping Handbook 1975,* 93–95.

"Captain Crouton and the Men of the Cha-Cha in Grant Madness." *Harpoon,* January 1975, 32–34.

"The Birth." *Way,* January–February 1975, 26–31.

"Crucifixion and Resurrection." *Our Family* [Canada], February 1975, 9–23. Photographs by Justin Soleta.

"The Black Cottonwood." *Pacific Wilderness Journal,* February–March 1975, 11.

"Mighty Chickadee." *National Wildlife,* April–May 1975, 32–33.

"To the Country and Back." *Lady's Circle,* June 1975, 38–39, 63.

"Rau's Wolf." *Sports Illustrated,* June 2, 1975, 88. [Letter to the editor.]

"Rare, Threatened and Endangered." *Register-Guard* [Eugene, OR], June 5, 1975, 1C.

"The Passing of the Night." *Audubon,* July 1975, 18–25.

Lopez approached the editors about developing a story on darkness as one more dwindling natural resource. His major essays, which had been appearing in *North American Review,* now began to appear in *Audubon* and soon will start appearing almost exclusively in *Harper's.*

"Fire Camp." *American Forests,* August 1975, 36–38.

In the summer of 1974 Lopez followed a Forest Service Hot Shot (fire suppression) crew from Redding, California, while they fought a 110,000-acre fire near Lake Chelan, Washington. Although the article he wrote was never published, his photographs of one of the fire camps appear here.

"My Horse." *North American Review,* Summer 1975, 8–10.

In the early seventies Lopez traveled extensively around the West in a three-quarter-ton Dodge van, which he had outfitted with a sleeping platform and a rudimentary cooking set-up. The essay, drawing on the relationship of some Native American warriors to their best horses, portrays this truck as the author's companion on several memorable drives. The piece has been reprinted more than twenty times, mostly in high school and university textbooks.

"National Bird . . . ?" *Register-Guard* [Eugene, OR], September 7, 1975, 3D–4D.

"A Jury of Your Peers." *Eugene,* November 1975, 20–23.

Lopez gave his support to this new city magazine, recalling his own days in 1968 when he co-founded and wrote for *Focus Michiana* in South Bend, Indiana. Here, he focuses on the process of jury selection and the notion of "one's peers."

"The Magical Waters of Oregon." *Travel & Leisure,* November 1975, W20f–W20h.

During his early years in Oregon Lopez visited nearly every part of the state. This was one of his first pieces for the magazine, and it drew heavily on the visual and emotional experiences of those trips.

"Scarface Visits the Sun." *Tales,* Fall 1975, no pagination.

"The Development of the Wolf in North America." *North American Review,* Fall 1975, 60–65. Photographs by John Bauguess.

In the early stages of his research for *Of Wolves and Men,* Lopez contacted editor Robley Wilson about publishing this unusual piece, a series of photographic layouts with text, Lopez's first attempts to create a suitable design for the book.

1976

"Coyote and Rattlesnake." *Northwest Review* 15.2 (1976), 12–17.

"The Deserts of the Great Basin Perceived." *Travel & Leisure,* May 1976, W14h, W60b.

By now, the author's long-standing practice, as here, of urging readers to look more closely at what is often overlooked in the natural world has become a familiar theme in his work.

"Wolves in the Lower 48." *Journal of the North American Wolf Society,* May 1976, 10–17.

Lopez met editor Sandra Gray during a period of research on wolves and was impressed with the seriousness of her approach to securing a more balanced public view of this animal's nature. Lopez wrote, in essence, a scientific research paper for her journal, about a controversial subject, the purported appearance of wolves in the lower 48 states in areas where they were believed to be extinct.

"Coyote and the Kalapuya Indians." *McKenzie Enterprise,* June 1–15, 1976, 1, 7. ["Coyote Gambles," "The Origin of Death," and "Coyote Takes Water from the Frog People," with an introductory note by Lopez.]

"Twilight." *North American Review,* Summer 1976, 4–5.

"Wolf Kill." *Harper's,* August 1976, 25–27.

Lopez's first article for *Harper's.*

"Three Striped, High-Heeled, Patent Leather Jogging Clogs." *Eugene,* September 1976, 28–33.

"Intentions in North America, the Buffalo." *Chouteau Review,* Fall–Winter 1976, 74–78. [Subsequently reprinted in *Winter Count* and elsewhere as "Buffalo."]

1977

"What are Wolves?" *Travel & Leisure,* January 1977, 6–8, 12.

"Alaska Gets Lift from Winter Blues." *Register-Guard* [Eugene, OR], February 27, 1977, 2D.

"Alaskan Journal." *Environmental Action,* June 18, 1977, 10–12.

"Travels with Fido." *Backpacker,* August 1977, 30–31.

"The Photographer." *North American Review,* Fall 1977, 66–67.

Lopez was a landscape photographer, 1965–81. This short story explores a theme that turns up repeatedly later in his fiction and nonfiction: the commercialization of environmental sentiments and the metaphysical qualities of photography. The accompanying photograph of a man's torso by Lopez is of his longtime friend Richard Showalter.

"An Alaskan Tragedy." *Harper's,* September 1977, 30–33.

Lopez's second essay for *Harper's.* He strongly disagreed with several changes the magazine made in order to make the piece more controversial.

"Woods Words." *Quest/77,* September–October 1977, 115.

Quest was founded by former members of the editorial staffs of *Harper's* and *Travel & Leisure* magazines, both of which Lopez was writing for. A distinguishing feature of the magazine was its "Potentials" section, sixteen pages devoted to a single topic. Here the topic was wood. Lopez wrote about the folk language of logging crews.

"In Search of Silence." *Travel & Leisure,* November 1977, 81–82.

"On the Preservation of Other Creatures." *Oregonians Cooperating to Protect Whales,* November–December 1977, 1–2.

"Wood I-Beams." *Popular Science,* December 1977, 92.

1978

"Coyote and Wolverine." *Dalmo'ma* 1.2 (1978), 10–11.

"The Indian's Cottonwood." *Minnesota Volunteer,* March–April 1978, 60–62.

"The Bull Rider." *Chouteau Review,* Spring 1978, 53–62.

"Three Trickster Stories." *Skywriting,* Spring 1978, 41–51. ["Coyote and His Knee," "Coyote Shows How He Can Lie," and "The Tree Holders," with commentary by Lopez.]

"The Creek." *Sierra,* May 1978, 29.

"Mill Lumber with Your Chain Saw." *Popular Science,* June 1978, 86–89, 184. With his friend Richard Showalter, a toy-maker and woodworker, Lopez purchased an Alaska mill, which they used to make lumber for various projects. The practical experience served as the basis for a contribution to the magazine, by now a familiar pattern in the author's freelance work.

"The American Indian Mind." *Quest/78,* Potentials section, September–October 1978, 109–24. With the help of editor Tony Jones, Lopez developed this sixteen-page section on Native American philosophy. He invited contributions from his former mentor, Barre Toelken, and from Robert Stephenson, an Alaskan wolf biologist whom Lopez had met in March 1976 and with whom he would travel extensively in Alaska. Lopez wrote many of the short pieces in this section and utilized a number of unpublished historical photographs provided by Richard Pohrt, Sr. The Chandler-Pohrt collection of Native American material culture was one of the most important such collections in the world. Lopez's friendship with the Pohrt family began with Richard Pohrt's oldest son, Karl, director of Bear Claw Press, which was publishing Howard Norman's early work and that of other writers with a serious interest in Native American culture. Lopez called on Karl and his father for guidance in the development of this special section, and it was during this time that he met the youngest of Pohrt's sons, Tom, who would later illustrate *Crow and Weasel.*

1979

"The Heart of the Matter." *Notre Dame Magazine,* February 1979, 26–31.

"Trying the Land." *Harper's,* February 1979, 96–97.

"Dave's Story: Five Dollar Dogs." *North American Review,* Spring 1979, 52–53.

"Grown Men." *Notre Dame Magazine,* October 1979, 17–19.

1980

"Wilderness and Natural Order." *Oregon Magazine,* January 1980, 62, 61.
[Editorial based on oral testimony before Senator Mark Hatfield in field
hearings on a federal wilderness bill, July 2, 1979, Pendleton, Oregon.]
These hearings were an effort by Oregon's outspoken and well-organized
environmental community to present to the senator a broad-based
rationale for the preservation of undisturbed landscapes. Lopez recalls
that the senator listened with utter indifference.

"A Presentation of Whales." *Harper's,* March 1980, 68–79.

"The Lover of Words." *North American Review,* Spring 1980, 25–27.

"Against the Earth: A Western Literature." *Jeopardy,* Winter 1980, 12–15.
An early attempt by Lopez to call attention to the history of landscape
literature in the American West. He had been invited to Western
Washington University to speak, and this was the students' literary
magazine.

1981

"Into the Earth: A Journey for the Soul." *Notre Dame Magazine,* May 1981,
30–34. [Subsequently reprinted in *Crossing Open Ground* and elsewhere as
"Gone Back into the Earth."]

"Murder: A Memoir." *Rocky Mountain Magazine,* May–June 1981, 58, 60. [A
rewritten version of this story appeared in *Oregon Quarterly* (1998) and in
About This Life.]

"The Elusive Mountain Lion." *GEO,* June 1981, 98–116.
This highly successful, environmentally sensitive German magazine
introduced an American version in 1980, edited by David Maxey.
Lopez felt a sense of camaraderie with him and was eager to write
for the magazine. Maxey suggested the American mountain lion as a
topic because of Lopez's long-standing interest in large predators. The
French and German "translations" of this article were so sentimentalized
that Lopez came to regret their publication under his name, as well
as subsequent "translations" of "A Staging of Snow Geese" (1982) that
appeared in the German and French *GEO.*

"In a Country of Light: Among Animals." *Outside,* June–July 1981, 36–45.

"How the Land Nourishes Nation's Writers." *Chicago Tribune,* July 26, 1981, 2 1–2.

"Borders." *Country Journal,* September 1981, 32, 34–36.

"The Man Who Had Maps." *North American Review,* September 1981, 32–33.

> "This was my first attempt to fictionalize an obsession that fascinates me—the collection and curation of maps. The second effort came twenty years later with 'The Mappist' (2000)."

"Laying It on the Line." *Running,* November–December 1981, 42–48.

> "Nike, the shoe manufacturer, turned its in-house publication into a trade magazine and hired Paul Perry to edit it. Perry asked me to work with him on stories that might be only peripherally concerned with running. This, the first of two pieces, was about a former classmate of mine, Hall of Fame football player Alan Page, who would later sit on the Minnesota Supreme Court. [The other story, 'One for the Heart' (1983), was about sled dogs.] Perry was a friend of John Rasmus, the editor of *Outside,* for whom I was also writing. The three of us would remain in regular touch for years as Perry and Rasmus moved on to edit other magazines for which I wrote."

1982

"A Faint Light on the Northern Edge." *North American Review,* March 1982, 12–21.

> An important essay, according to Lopez, about hunting with traditional people on St. Lawrence Island in the northern Bering Sea. It grew out of a trip he had made to the island with wolf biologist and close friend Robert Stephenson. The epilogue to *Arctic Dreams* was based on the same trip.

"Out of a Desert Landscape: Open Spaces and the Human Spirit." *American West,* March–April 1982, 50–55.

> "This piece marks my first formal exploration of Wallace Stegner's notion that a person is shaped by the landscape he or she grows up in."

"Children in the Woods." *Pacific Northwest,* April 1982, 8.

"Yukon-Charley and the Dimensions of Wilderness." *Wilderness,* Fall 1982, 24–31. [Subsequently reprinted under this title and, in *Crossing Open Ground* and elsewhere, as "Yukon-Charley: The Shape of Wilderness."]

"A Staging of Snow Geese." *Outside,* October 1982, 42–46, 74–76.

> [Subsequently reprinted under this title and as "A Reflection on White Geese."]
>
> Selected for *The Best of Outside* [Magazine]*: The First 20 Years* (1997).

"The Lives of Seals." *Science/82,* November 1982, 50–55.

1983

"One for the Heart." *Running,* January–February 1983, 34–39.

"Alaska's Teeming Wildlife." *New York Times,* March 13, 1983, "Travel" department, 9, 29.

> One of several newspaper and magazine pieces Lopez wrote from the research he was doing for *Arctic Dreams.*

"Searching for Ancestors." *Outside,* April 1983, 74–77, 84–86.

> Lopez was by now a correspondent at the magazine.

"Renegotiating the Contracts." *Parabola,* May 1983, 14–19. [A production error caused the fourteenth paragraph of this essay to be published as its final paragraph. The correct version appears for the first time in *This Incomperable Lande* (1989), edited by Thomas J. Lyon.]

> The editors of *Parabola* invited Lopez to help on a special issue about animals. He did, and also wrote this essay about the kind of ethical relationships with animals that he believes must be a part of any successful reorganization of American society and its politics.

"The Dark Road." *Outside,* November 1983, 70–71.

> The first of three pieces Lopez would write about road-killed animals—the daily toll of deaths, society's indifference, and what the magnitude of the slaughter says about us as a culture. The others are "Apologia" (1989) and "Implacable Corridors of Death" (1992).

1984

"Ravens." *American West,* January–February 1984, 80–81.

> According to Lopez, this "barely qualifies" as poetry. It is his only published poem, aside from "Desert Reservation," which Copper Canyon Press issued as a chapbook in 1980.

"Out Here Spring Is for Rediscovery." *Washington Post,* March 25, 1984, C1–C2.

"Class Notes." *North American Review,* June 1984, 40–41. [Attributed to Lucas Cooper, pseud. for Barry Lopez.]

> Bothered by the relentlessly upbeat tone of the class notes section in alumni magazines, Lopez employs the form here to chronicle the breakdowns, betrayals, and suffering that are as characteristic of human existence as news items about corporate advancement and professional awards.

"A Short Manifesto." *Women in the Wilderness,* Fall–Winter 1984, 4. [Newsletter.]

> First appearance in a periodical for this short essay, Lopez's contribution to a broadside project by Copper Canyon Press (1984).

"Story at Anaktuvuk Pass." *Harper's,* December 1984, 49–52. [Subsequently reprinted in *Crossing Open Ground* and elsewhere as "Landscape and Narrative."]

1985

"The Passing Wisdom of Birds." *Orion Nature Quarterly,* Autumn 1985, 15–21.
The second of more than a dozen of Lopez's pieces that will appear in the magazine. The first was a book review in 1984.
Selected as a Notable Essay, *The Best American Essays 1986.*
"The Medicines." *Chouteau Review,* Fall 1985, 49–50.

1986

"The Great Green North." *Vogue,* June 1986, 152, 154.
"*Vogue* invited me to write this travel piece. However, the magazine's primary fixation on what is fashionable—the art editor cut the story's opening paragraph at the last minute to make room for a larger image—made this, I was sorry to have to say, a one-story relationship with them."
"The Stone Horse." *Antaeus,* Autumn 1986, 220–29.
Selected for *The Best American Essays 1987.*
"Japan's True North." *New York Times Magazine,* October 5, 1986, 36–37, 82, 84, 86, 88–89. [Subsequently reprinted in *About This Life* as "A Short Passage in Northern Hokkaido."]
"Uncle Wiggily's Karma and Other Childhood Memories." *New York Times Book Review,* December 7, 1986, 46.
Untitled contribution to a section of comments by twenty authors on books that influenced them as children.

1987

"California Desert: A Worldly Wilderness." *National Geographic,* January 1987, 42–77.
"I was skeptical about working with the magazine because of its history, in my view, of bemusement with indigenous peoples and its disregard for the place of women in human societies. At the urging of Charles McCarry, however, I took an assignment to write about the California portions of the Sonora and Mojave deserts. It was a satisfactory experience and I regret I was not able to make room in my schedule to write more for McCarry."
Selected for *From the Field,* an anthology of the best writing from the first one hundred years of *National Geographic.*

"Landscapes Open and Closed." *Harper's,* July 1987, 51–58.

> Lopez calls this "a pivotal piece for me." Before departing on a long journey through unpopulated landscapes in southern Africa, he attended a federal proceeding in Delmas, South Africa, where nineteen middle-aged black men were on trial for sedition. In this major essay for *Harper's,* he contends that he no longer wants to sojourn in the wild without the knowledge of trials like this at the center of his thoughts. Further, he hopes those relentlessly focused on the trial will come to understand the human need to make contemplative journeys into "unsettled" country, far removed from the social and political violence that gave rise to the Delmas trial.
>
> Selected as a Notable Essay, *The Best American Essays 1988.*

"Treasured Places." *Life,* July 1987, 40–42.

> By this time, a large national audience had developed for the kinds of ideas Lopez and other writers had been espousing for a decade and a half concerning the relationship of society to place. The magazine commissioned photographs of several of the major contributors to this movement—Edward Hoagland, Galen Rowell, Ed Abbey, James Dickey, and Peter Matthiessen—and asked the authors to write brief opinion pieces. In the layout, Lopez is seen standing on a boulder in the middle of the McKenzie River in front of his Oregon home.

1988

"Trouble Way Down Under." *Washington Post,* March 27, 1988, C1, C2.

> The first of ten pieces Lopez will write on Antarctica.

"Standing on the South Pole." *Washington Post,* March 27, 1988, C2.

> One of several pieces to come out of Lopez's first journey to Antarctica (two more are cited immediately above and below). In defiance of the tradition of planting flags in remote places, Lopez flies a kite at the geographic South Pole and reports on scientific research at America's Amundsen-Scott South Pole Station.

"Informed by Indifference: A Walk in Antarctica." *Harper's,* May 1988, 66–68.

> Selected as a Notable Essay, *The Best American Essays 1989.*

"A Chinese Garland: Charles Wright, Barry Lopez, Maxine Hong Kingston." *North American Review,* September 1988, 38–42. [Lopez, pp. 41–42.]

> Lopez was one of twelve writers invited to China to make presentations to the Chinese Writers' Association in Leshan, Sichuan Province, in 1988. The party also traveled to Beijing, Xian, Chongqing, Wuhan, Chengdu,

and Shanghai. Lopez contacted Robley Wilson, the editor of *North American Review*, about the possibility of publishing some of the writers' formal remarks.

1989

"Our Frail Planet in Cold, Clear View." *Harper's*, May 1989, 43–49.

On his second trip to Antarctica, Lopez worked with glacial chemists camped in the Transantarctic Mountains and on the Polar Plateau, thirteen miles from the South Pole. An early report on the specter of climate change.

Selected as a Notable Essay, *The Best American Essays 1990*.

"Life and Death in Galápagos." *North American Review*, June 1989, 8–13.

[Subsequently reprinted in *About This Life* and elsewhere as "Orchids on the Volcanoes."]

Selected as a Notable Essay, *The Best American Essays 1990*.

"The American Geographies." *Orion Nature Quarterly*, Autumn 1989, 52–61.

This often reprinted essay was originally commissioned by Robert Atwan for *Openings: Original Essays by Contemporary Soviet and American Writers* (1990). It has occasionally been reprinted under an incorrect title, "Losing Our Sense of Place."

Recipient of an annual award from the National Council on Geographic Education and selected for *Finding Home* (1992), an anthology of the best writing from the first ten years of *Orion* magazine.

"Galápagos Rescue." *Defenders*, September–October 1989, 10–12.

On one of a series of trips to this archipelago, Lopez discovered more than a dozen sea lions trapped in a net, set illegally to snare and drown the animals. The carcasses were to be used as bait to attract sharks, to be killed illegally for their fins. With the help of Orlando Falco, a guide, Lopez reached the drowning animals in a small boat and proceeded to cut them free of the net. All but one, apparently, survived. Lopez revisits the incident in "Madre de Dios" (2008).

"Night Walking." *Walking Magazine*, October 1989, 80.

On a moonless night Lopez led a friend on a walk through the forest from an isolated and abandoned cabin (see "A Quiet Voice in the Wilderness," 1973) to his home. "Having walked the trail many times in daylight, I believed it would be possible to walk it in complete darkness, by feel alone."

"Apologia." *Witness* 3.4 (Winter 1989), 75–79.

Artist Robin Eschner later created twenty-three wood block prints to accompany this widely reprinted essay. The prints form a continuous image and were turned into a fine press limited edition book under the supervision of Charles Hobson at his Pacific Editions press. Lopez worked with both Eschner and Hobson on subsequent projects, and a trade version of Hobson's fine press book was published by the University of Georgia Press in 1998.

Selected by *Witness* for its special issue *Our Best 1987–2004*, 18.2 (2004). Selected as a Notable Essay, *The Best American Essays 1990*.

1990

"Edward Abbey: Eulogy." *Journal of Energy, Natural Resources and Environmental Law* 11.1 (January 1990), 16–18.

Transcript of a speech delivered at a memorial service for Edward Abbey outside Moab, Utah, May 20, 1989.

"Unbounded Wilderness." *Aperture,* Late Summer 1990, 2, 14.

Lopez's long involvement with photographers led to this invitation from the magazine's editor, Michael Hoffman, to write an introduction for an issue devoted to the theme "Beyond Wilderness." Work by several of Lopez's friends, including Gary Braasch and Stuart Klipper, appears in the issue.

"Jordan Valley, 1977." *Zyzzyva,* Summer 1990, 29–41.

"I often stopped in this small town in eastern Oregon for a meal. The town haunted me, and it is the setting for this story about a father and a son."

"Discovering the Americas, Again." *New York Times,* October 12, 1990, A17.

With the approach of the quincentennial of Columbus's landfall, Lopez wrote several pieces focused on a reconsideration of that event. In addition to this op-ed piece, he wrote *The Rediscovery of North America* (University Press of Kentucky, 1991) and surveyed twelve books about Columbus written for children in "Columbus for the Imagination," written for *The New York Times Book Review* (1991).

1991

"Faith in the Light: The Photography of Robert Adams." *Northwest Review* 29.2 (1991), 33–36. Photographs by Robert Adams, pp. 37–45.

A written version of a talk Lopez gave in January 1990 at the opening of a retrospective show of Adams's work at the Amon Carter Museum, Fort Worth, Texas.

"Remembering Orchards." *Oregonian* [Portland], Northwest Magazine
section, January 6, 1991, 20–21.

The story, published here for the first time, was subsequently selected for
a 1990 PEN/Syndicated Short Fiction Prize.

"Farewell to the Environment." *Buzzworm,* March–April 1991, 16. [One of
several short comments from authors gathered under this general title].

"A Very Personal Hospitality." *New York Times Magazine,* "The Sophisticated
Traveler" department, October 20, 1991, 10, 12. ["A White-Water River in
Oregon" is among several short contributions by various authors.]

"Making Animals Dance." *Outside,* November 1991, 20. [Letter to the editor.]
In his regular column, "Natural Acts," Lopez's friend David Quammen
raised questions about the meaning of zoos. Lopez took the opportunity
to write the magazine, supporting the column and praising Quammen
for addressing the subject.

"Invocation." OAC News [Oregon Arts Commission], Winter 1991, 16.

Lopez's invocation at the inauguration of Barbara Roberts as Governor of
Oregon, January 14, 1991, in Salem, Oregon.

1992

"The Gift of Good Land." *Antarctic Journal of the United States,* June 1992, 1–4.

The National Science Foundation invited Lopez to deliver this keynote
address at the dedication of the Creary Laboratory at McMurdo Station,
Antarctica, in November 1991.

"The Rediscovery of North America." *Orion,* Summer 1992, 10–16.

The written version of a talk Lopez presented in November 1989 at the
University of Kentucky. [Subsequently published in book form by the
University Press of Kentucky as the first Thomas D. Clark Lecture, it
appeared here for the first time in a periodical.]

Chosen as a Notable Essay, *The Best American Essays 1993.*

"Nature-Writing Symposium: The Rise of Nature Writing, America's Next
Great Genre? Rick Bass, John Daniels . . . Barry Lopez . . . [and others]
Respond to John A. Murray." *Manoa,* Fall 1992, 72–96. [Lopez, pp.
89–90.]

"Benjamin Claire, North Dakota Tradesman, Writes to the President of the
United States." *North American Review,* September–October 1992, 16–20.

"For many years I held onto an image of a child leading an enormous
battleship through the air on a string, like a balloon. The image, along
with my concern about our country's capitulation to George H. W.

Bush's Middle East policy which led to the Gulf War, compelled this story." This is one of five short stories Lopez has set in North Dakota. The others are "Restoration," in *Winter Count* (1981); "The Interior of North Dakota," in *The Paris Review* (1992); "In the Great Bend of the Souris River," in *Manoa* (1997); and "The Mappist," in *The Georgia Review* (2000). "Whenever I travel through this region," Lopez says, "I'm struck by the country's layers of timelessness and obscurity."

"Implacable Corridors of Death," *Los Angeles Times*, October 4, 1992, M5.
Another effort, after the publication of "Apologia" in 1989, to address road kill, one of Lopez's recurrent subjects.

"The Interior of North Dakota." *Paris Review*, Winter 1992, 134–44.
Selected for *The Paris Review Book of Heartbreak, Madness* . . . (2003), an anthology of the magazine's best writing, 1953–2003.

1993

"Into the Ice." *American Way*, January 15, 1993, 58–62, 80, 85–86.
This recounting of a journey Lopez made to the Weddell Sea in the austral fall of 1991 anticipated the publication of a major essay on the same topic that Lopez had agreed to write for *Harper's*. Having lost the right of first appearance, *Harper's* declined, and the planned longer essay, "Offshore," was later published in *Orion* (1994).

"Replacing Memory." *Georgia Review* 47.1 (Spring 1993), 23–38.
Chosen for the journal's *Selected Essays 1947–1996* [double issue, Winter 2001–Spring 2002], selected for *American Nature Writing 1994*, and chosen as a Notable Essay, *The Best American Essays 1994*.

"The Hitter." *North American Review*, July–August 1993, 32–34.
A short story about two professional baseball players who leave baseball and live as a couple in the fifties. One of them is tracked down by an obsessive and disturbed fan who resents the ballplayer's early retirement from the sport.

"Writer, Storyteller, Healer." *PEN Newsletter*, October 1993, 4.
Lopez wrote this brief piece in response to a request from PEN. It is a succinct statement of beliefs he often sets forth, particularly at his readings and lectures, about what it means to him to be a writer.

"Thomas Lowdermilk's Generosity." *American Short Fiction*, Winter 1993, 36–46.
Chosen for Honorable Mention in *The Best American Short Fiction 1994*.

1994

"Rubén Mendoza Vega, Suzuki Professor of Early Caribbean History,
University of Florida at Gainesville, Offers a History of the United States
Based on Personal Experience." *Manoa,* Summer 1994, 43–49.

This is Lopez's first story for the journal. In 2006 he will become a
corresponding editor and with Frank Stewart subsequently co-edit three
issues, *Where the Rivers Meet: New Writing from Australia* (2006), *Maps of
Reconciliation: Literature and the Ethical Imagination* (2007), and *Gates of
Reconciliation: Literature and the Ethical Imagination* (2008).

"The Entreaty of the Wiideema." *North American Review,* July–August 1994,
35–38.

Selected for *The Year's Best Fantasy and Horror, Eighth Annual Collection*
(1995).

"In Memoriam, Wallace Stegner." *Portland,* Autumn 1994, 20–21.

Based on one of two talks Lopez gave about the meaning of Stegner's
work and vision, this one at the University of Portland. The other was
"Looking in the Deeper Lair: A Tribute to Wallace Stegner" (1995),
presented at the Herbst Theater in San Francisco.

"Pearyland." *Outside,* September 1994, 94–98, 156.

"Offshore: A Journey to the Weddell Sea." *Orion,* Winter 1994, 48–65.

An essay about the initial voyage of the *Nathanial B. Palmer,* an ice-
breaking research vessel, from the coast of Louisiana to the Weddell Sea.
It was the first vessel to enter those waters in winter since the crushing of
Shackleton's *Endurance* there in 1916. The themes of long-distance travel and
the technical sophistication of the ship paralleled, in Lopez's mind, similar
themes in "Flight" too closely to warrant including it in *About This Life.*
Selected for *American Nature Writing 1995.*

"Rare Companions: Endangered Species of North America." *Orion,* Winter
1994, 33. Photographs by Susan Middleton and David Liittschwager,
commentary by Barry Lopez. See "Landscapes of the Shamans" (2013).

A tribute to the work of two photographers whose dedication and vision
Lopez found inspiring, part of an expanding effort by the author at this
time to promote the work of other writers and artists.

1995

"Occupancy." *Orion,* Spring 1995. [Reprint of Morning Star Press broadside,
redesigned as double-folded broadside, 15.5 × 20.75 inches, and tipped in
between pp. 41–42.]

In collaboration with Scottish publisher Alec Finlay, Lopez drew this map of his homeplace on the McKenzie River and wrote a brief, incorporated essay. *Orion* had expressed a strong interest in finding a way to circulate this broadside to a wider audience in the United States.

"Caring for the Woods." *Audubon,* March–April 1995, 58–60, 62–63.

Lopez's first appearance in the magazine since 1975, an essay about the responsibilities of land ownership and the caretaking of his home landscape in Oregon's Cascade Mountains.

Selected for *American Nature Writing* 1996 and chosen as a Notable Essay, *The Best American Essays 1996.*

"Looking in the Deeper Lair: A Tribute to Wallace Stegner. *Northern Lights* 11.2 (Summer 1995), 28–29.

Published as a fine press limited edition book by lone goose press, Eugene, Oregon, 1996. At this point, Lopez changed the wording of the title from "the deeper lair" to "a deeper lair." Selected for *The Pushcart Prize XXI: Best of the Small Presses 1997.*

"Lopez–Lanting: A Collaboration." *Audubon,* July–August 1995, 68–75.

Lopez and a longtime friend and colleague, photographer Frans Lanting, first worked together on "A Staging of Snow Geese" (1982) and in the mid-nineties produced a series of wall calendars combining work that each had previously published.

"Suffering in Silence for the Home of the Cougar and the Bear." *Oregonian* [Portland], August 27, 1995, B1, B4. [Subsequently reprinted as "Natural Grief."]

"In this op-ed piece I suggest that grief at the death of a loved one comes closer to describing many people's feelings about industrial logging than the emotions of either depression or despair."

"On the Wings of Commerce." *Harper's,* October 1995, 39–54. [Subsequently reprinted as "Flight" in *About This Life* and elsewhere.]

1996

"A Literature of Place." *Heat* [Australia] 2 (1996), 52–58.

First publication of a written version of a talk Lopez delivered in Hobart, Australia, in March 1996 at the Salamanca Writers Conference. The first North American publication (other than e-journal) was in *Portland* (1997). An unauthorized edit of the essay, entitled "We Are Shaped by the Sound of the Wind, the Slant of Sunlight," appeared later in *High Country News* and was subsequently reprinted elsewhere.

"At the Altar, Boy." *Portland,* Spring 1996, 17.

One of several pieces Lopez has written on spiritual themes for friend and editor Brian Doyle and this prize-winning alumni magazine. Doyle and Lopez both attended the University of Portland's sister school, Notre Dame.

"The Outside Canon: A Few Great Books." *Outside,* May 1996, 66–80.

Lopez contributed a brief review (p. 76) of *Libyan Sands: Travel in a Dead World,* by Ralph Bagnold, to this compendium of more than one hundred books.

"Jedidiah Speaks with the River." *Orion,* Summer 1996, 26–28.

A short story inspired in part by Lopez's daily habit of visiting the stretch of the McKenzie River in front of his home. He has used this setting and the emotions it provokes in him in several other pieces, including "Empira's Tapestry" in *Field Notes,* "The Naturalist" in *Orion* (2001), and "Waiting for Salmon" (2005), an essay, in *Granta.*

"In the Garden of the Lords of War." *Manoa,* Summer 1996, 54–58.

Selected for *American Nature Writing 1997.*

"Mornings in Quarain." *Gettysburg Review* 9.4 (Autumn 1996), 659–65.

"Searching for Depth in Bonaire." *Georgia Review* 50.3 (Fall 1996), 545–58.

Selected for *American Nature Writing 1998* and as a Notable Essay, *The Best American Essays 1997.*

1997

"My Hands." *Men's Journal,* December 1996–January 1997, 98–102, 136.

[Subsequently reprinted in *About This Life* and elsewhere as "A Passage of the Hands."]

"A Literature of Place." *Portland,* Summer 1997, 22–25.

The first U.S. publication of an essay that originally appeared in the Australian journal *Heat.*

"The Letters of Heaven." *Georgia Review* 51.3 (Fall 1997), 497–507.

A finalist for the National Magazine Award in Fiction and chosen for Honorable Mention in *The Best American Short Fiction 1998.*

"Rediscovering Animals." *Inside Borders,* December 1997, 17.

A short piece about how animals have served storytellers for millennia, and why they should not be viewed as subjects solely of interest to children. Written for the in-house magazine of the Borders chain of book stores.

"Ferocious Love." *Portland,* Winter 1997, 26–27. [Subsequently reprinted as

"God's Love on a Darkling Plain."]
Selected for *The Best Spiritual Writing 1998.*
"In the Great Bend of the Souris River." *Manoa,* Winter 1997, 113–18.
"Michio Hoshino: A Tribute." *Orion,* Winter 1997, 38–39.
> "The photographer Hoshino and I corresponded but never met. When Hoshino was killed by a grizzly bear on Russia's Kamchatka Peninsula, I wrote this tribute."

1998

"Before the Temple of Fire." *Harper's,* January 1998, 35–50. [Subsequently reprinted in *About This Life* as "Effleurage, The Stroke of Fire."]
"Revelations." *Story,* Spring 1998, 42–45.
> When Lois Rosenthal, editor of the magazine, heard Lopez's first public reading from an early draft of his book-length manuscript "Encounters on the Granite River" at the Bread Loaf Writers' Conference in 1997, she asked if she could publish several of its fifty-two brief stories. The book is divided into four sections, each one standing for a season and consisting of thirteen stories. Four stories appear here, one from each season. The full manuscript has not been published as a book.

"Learning to See." *DoubleTake,* Spring 1998, 73–79.
"Murder: A Memoir." *Oregon Quarterly,* Spring 1998, 14–16. [A rewritten version of a story by the same title that appeared previously in *Rocky Mountain Magazine* (1981).]
"The Whaleboat." *Outside,* May 1998, 142–48, 196–98.
> Selected as a Notable Essay, *The Best American Essays 1999.*

"The Language of Animals." *Wild Earth,* Summer 1998, inside front cover, 2–6.
> A widely reprinted essay on Lopez's familiar theme of the otherness of animals, originally written for *World Views and the American West* (2002), a festschrift celebrating the work of his mentor Barre Tolken.
> Selected for *Best Spiritual Writing 1999* and for *Only Connect: Soil, Soul, Society, The Best of Resurgence Magazine* [England] *1990–1999.*

"Two Dogs at Rowena." *American Way,* July 1, 1998, 44–47, 120–21.
> "When John Fowles visited Oregon, I took him to the Columbia River Gorge to look for orchids, a passion of his. We passed an hour at a prominent headland called Rowena. The story was generated by the wonder, mystery, and melancholy of our search that day."

1999

"A Most Compelling Vista." *Portland,* Summer 1999, 21.

"The Deaf Girl." *Story* 47.4 (Autumn 1999), 109–12.

"Antarctica." *National Geographic Traveler,* October 1999, 109–10.

"Emory Bear Hands' Birds." *Island* [Australia], Winter 1999, 48–55.

> First English-language publication of this story. First North American publication is in *San Francisco* (2000).

"A Passage of Seasons." *Orion,* Winter 1999, 63–71. Illustrations by Ladislav Hanka.

> Twelve stories—Lopez sometimes refers to them as "revelations"—from an early draft of his "Encounters on the Granite River," a book-length fiction manuscript of fifty-two brief stories, three from each of the book's four sections.

2000

"Confessions." *Paris Review,* Winter 1999–2000, 154–56.

> A very brief work of fiction, this is Lopez's contribution to the PEN/ Faulkner fundraising gala at the Folger Library in Washington, D.C., in 1997. Each year a dozen or so writers are asked to compose and read three minutes of prose or poetry on a common theme, that year's being "Confessions." Lopez's story (called "Restitution" but retitled "Confessions" here) accompanies work by seventeen other writers from the first eight years of PEN's annual gala, under the general title "Three Minutes or Less."

["Nights in Antarctica."] *National Geographic Adventure,* January–February 2000, 124. [Appears under department heading "Journal," without title.]

"Stolen Horses." In *Writers Harvest 3,* edited by Tobias Wolff, 145–52. New York: Dell, 2000.

"Emory Bear Hands' Birds." *San Francisco,* May 2000, 82–85, 131.

> This is the first U.S. publication of a short story that originally appeared in the Australian journal *Island.*

"The Mappist." *Georgia Review* 54.1 (Spring 2000), 45–55.

"The Near Woods." *Seneca Review,* Spring 2000, 100–102.

> Editor John D'Agata asked Lopez for an original contribution to this thirtieth anniversary issue, celebrating the lyric essay.

"Eliminations." *The Yale Literary Magazine* 12.2 (Fall 2000), 28.

> A brief essay about endangered languages, especially those that have

become extinct in the United States. Part of a special section of lists compiled by invited writers.

"The Himalayan Parchment." *Brick* [Canada], Fall 2000, 153–56.

Lopez submitted this short story to one of Canada's leading literary magazines after meeting editor Linda Spalding when they read together in Toronto. He intended to include it in the short story collection *Light Action in the Caribbean*, but he deleted it in the final edit.

"Hope amid Battle Stories." *SEJournal*, Winter 2000, 12–13.

Written version of a keynote address delivered to the Society of Environmental Journalists at Santa Barbara, California, September 1999.

2001

"Our Addiction to Oil, Our Making and Our Undoing." *Oregonian* [Portland], March 25, 2001, D1, D2.

Originally titled "Adolescence" and written for *Arctic Refuge: A Circle of Testimony* (2001).

"What to Carry." *Portland*, Spring 2001, 18.

A commencement address at Texas Tech University, December 2000.

"The Naturalist." *Orion*, Autumn 2001, 38–43.

An often reprinted essay, written at the request of friend and editor Emerson Blake for a special issue on natural history.

Selected for *Best American Spiritual Writing 2002* and chosen as a Notable Essay, *The Best American Essays 2002*.

2002

"A Scary Abundance of Water." *LA Weekly*, January 11–17, 2002, 26–29, 31–34.

"This is a memoir of my childhood, of growing up in California's San Fernando Valley at a time of transition from small-scale agriculture to suburban housing."

Nominated for the Pulitzer Prize in Feature Writing and chosen as a Notable Essay, *The Best American Essays 2003*.

"Steinbeck's Influence." In *John Steinbeck: Centennial Reflections by American Writers*, edited by Susan Shillinglaw, 57–61. San Jose, CA: Center for Steinbeck Studies, San Jose State University, 2002.

2003

"Pulling Wire." *Iron Horse Literary Review* 5.1 (First Frost 2003), 37–41.

"Speak up Now against the War in Iraq." *Oregonian* [Portland], February 13, 2003, C11.

"Southern Navigation." *Georgia Review* 57.3 (Fall 2003), 547–62.

> Lopez backtracks on Shackleton's journey from South Georgia to Elephant Island, encountering heavy weather in the Drake Passage along the way and reflecting on the safety and emotional distance his tour ship provides.
>
> Chosen as a Notable Essay, *The Best American Essays 2004.*

"Imagination and the Wild Cards of History." *Resource Lines* 14.1 (December 2003), 1, 3.

> A commencement address, delivered at Utah State University, June 2003.

2005

"Waiting for Salmon." *Granta,* Summer 2005, 75-84.

> A personal reflection on global warming and climate change. Salmon spawning in front of Lopez's Oregon home, 1970–2004, provide the essay's central point of reference.
>
> Chosen as a Notable Essay, *The Best American Essays 2006.*

2006

"Eden Is a Conversation." *Portland* 25.3 (Autumn 2006), 23.

> Adapted from a talk delivered at the Quest for Global Healing international gathering in Ubud, Bali, May 2006.

2007

"The Leadership Imperative: An Interview with Oren Lyons by Barry Lopez." *Orion,* January–February 2007, 36–43.

"Coldscapes." *National Geographic* 212.6 (December 2007), 136–55.

"Editor's Note." *Manoa,* Winter 2007, vii–ix.

> The first of two consecutive issues of the journal co-edited by Lopez and editor Frank Stewart and devoted to the theme of reconciliation, with original work from writers in various countries. This issue is titled "Maps of Reconciliation: Literature and the Ethical Imagination."

2008

"¡Nunca Más!" *Manoa,* Summer 2008, vii–xii.

> This essay was commissioned by the French national-circulation daily newspaper *Libération* and published in French in June 2006. The English-language version was accepted for publication by *Manoa.* Before it appeared there, it was published in a fine press limited edition by Red Dragonfly Press (2007).

"Epilogue." *Manoa,* Summer 2008, 171–72.

> Lopez wrote the closing note for the second of two issues of the journal devoted to the theme of reconciliation, this one titled "Gates of Reconciliation: Literature and the Ethical Imagination." See "Editor's Note" (2007).

"Reading the West: Writers' Advice for the Next President." *Santa Fe Reporter,* September 24–30, 2008, 17–24.

> Jeff Lee, director of the Rocky Mountain Land Library in Denver, Colorado, asked writers living in the western states to create a primer on the American West for the president-elect. The recommendations of thirteen writers were prepared as a handout for attendees at the Democratic National Convention in Denver in 2008. An edited version of this list, with additional contributions from other writers in the West, appeared in the September 9, 2008 edition of *High Country News.* The unedited contributions of the original thirteen writers were published by *The Reporter* of Santa Fe, New Mexico.

"Madre de Dios." *Portland* 27.4 (Winter 2008), 26–29.

> Selected for *Best American Essays 2009* and recipient of a silver medal from the National Council for the Advancement and Support of Education.

2009

"Call from the Future." *O, The Oprah Magazine,* April 2009, 156.

"Hidian." *TriQuarterly,* Spring 2009, 79–84.

"Notes from the Earth." *The American Scholar,* Autumn 2009, 43–49.

> Selected for *Best Spiritual Writing 2011.* See "An Intimate Geography" (2010).

"On the Border." *The Georgia Review,* Fall 2009, 373–80.

2010

"The Trail." *Orion,* January–February 2010, 49.

> Selected for *The Best American Nonrequired Reading 2010.*

"Dixon Marsh." *Orion,* July–August 2010, 42–45.

"A Dark Light in the West: Racism and Reconciliation." *The Georgia Review,* 64.3 (Fall 2010), 365–86.

"An Intimate Geography." *Portland,* Summer 2010 (29.2), 30–35.

> Published here with unauthorized *American Scholar* edits removed and original language and title restored. It is this version of the essay that appears in *Best Spiritual Writing 2011.*

"Six Thousand Lessons." *Kyoto Journal,* no. 75 (2010), 10–11.

2011

"The Museum of Game Balls." *Manoa,* January 2011, 97–105.

2013

"Sliver of Sky: Confronting the Trauma of Sexual Abuse." *Harper's,* January 2013, 41–48.

Lopez writes here in detail about his experience with childhood sexual abuse and his lifelong effort to deal with these years of trauma. He refers briefly to these events in two earlier autobiographical essays, "Madre de Dios" (2008) and "A Scary Abundance of Water" (2002).

"Perth, Outpost at the Edge." *Newsweek,* April 12, 2013. http:// www.thedailybeast.com/newsweek/2013/04/15/perth-outpost-at-the -edge-of-australia.html

"Landscapes of the Shamans." *Orion,* July–August 2013, 32–41.

Lopez speculates here that in recent years a new and fundamentally different view of wild animals has emerged in art. Accompanying the essay are illustrations of the work of installation artist Jane Alexander; photographers Lukas Felzmann, Frans Lanting, Wayne Levin, and Susan Middleton; painter Tom Uttech; and artists Sylvie Rosenthal and Rick Bartow.

Book Reviews

Too Far to Walk, by John Hersey. *Ave Maria,* March 26, 1966, 27–28.

Listen, Pilgrim, by Christopher Jones. *Ave Maria,* 20 January 1968, 25, 30.

"I came upon this book by accident, but my positive review elicited a letter from Jones, a 'street priest' of the time. We corresponded until Jones's death in 1974."

Evolution and Christian Hope, by Ernst Benz. *Ave Maria,* May 4, 1968, 26–27.

Look Around, Pilgrim, by Christopher Jones. *Ave Maria,* September 14, 1968, 27–29.

"Sports Illustrated Editor Takes a Balanced Look at Predator Issue." Rev. of *Slaughter the Animals, Poison the Earth,* by Jack Olsen. *Register-Guard* [Eugene, OR], Emerald Empire Magazine section, October 17, 1971, 8.

How to Keep Your Volkswagen Alive, by John Muir. *Popular Imported Cars,* November 1971, 37, 59.

"Catalog Provides Look at Oregon 'Characters.'" Rev. of *Catalog of Manuscripts in the University of Oregon Library,* by Martin Schmitt. *Register-Guard* [Eugene, OR], Emerald Empire Magazine section, December 19, 1971, 5.

Desert Solitaire, by Edward Abbey. *Not Man Apart,* May 1972, 15.
Selected for *Earthworks: Ten Years on the Environmental Front* (1980),
edited by Mary Lou Van Deventer, an anthology of the best writing
from *Not Man Apart,* 1970–79.

"Who's Expert on What at U of O." Rev. of *Register of Faculty Professional
Interests, University of Oregon,* ERIC Clearinghouse on Educational
Management. *Register-Guard* [Eugene, OR], Emerald Empire Magazine
section, February 23, 1973, 7.

"Ride 'em Cowboy." Rev. of *Let 'er Buck*, by Douglas Kent Hall. *Register-
Guard* [Eugene, OR], Emerald Empire Magazine section, November 18,
1973, 6.

Winter in the Blood, by James Welch. *Register-Guard* [Eugene, OR], April 7,
1975, 6C.

"Where the Wild Things Are." Rev. of *Cult of the Wild*, by Boyce Rensberger,
and *Animals and the Development of Human Intelligence*, by Paul Shepard.
Harper's, February 1978, 84–86, 90.

Keepers of the Game, by Calvin Martin. *Harper's,* December 1978, 82–83.
This rare praiseworthy attempt to bring the ethical philosophy behind
Native American hunting to the attention of a larger audience compelled
Lopez to approach *Harper's* about a review.

"Creatures Wild and Tame." Rev. of *Time of the Turtle*, by Jack Rudloe; *The
North Runner*, by R. D. Lawrence; *Wolves of Minong*, by Durward Allen;
and *Lure of the Dolphin*, by Robin Brown. *New York Times Book Review,*
July 22, 1979, 12–13.

"Allies on the Field." Rev. of *The Sinking Ark*, by Norman Myers. *Oregon
Magazine,* August 1980, 66–67.

"The Woods as the Refuge of the Unconscious." Rev. of *The Tree*, by John
Fowles. *Sierra,* September–October 1980, 64–67.
"I wanted to write this review because I thought Fowles's essay a succinct
and wise reflection on living with nature. I admired the essay and
thought the photographs that accompanied it were remarkable."

"Good Medicine from the High Buttes.*"* Rev. of *The Seven Visions of Bull
Lodge*, edited by George Horse Capture. *Pacific Northwest,* June 1981,
51–52.
The book's publisher, Bear Claw Press, was established by Lopez's friend
Karl Pohrt. Lopez admired both George Horse Capture's efforts to revive
Gros Ventre cultural tradition and the Pohrt family's long-term efforts to
promote Native American tradition and thought.

Indian Running, by Peter Nabokov. *Parabola*, January 1982, 106, 108.

The Biology of People, by Sam Singer and Henry R. Hilgard. *Outside*, April 1983, 108.

"This book was recommended to me by Lloyd Lowry, a biologist I traveled with while working on *Arctic Dreams*. The book had a major impact on my understanding of the need to take human biology more deeply into consideration in environmental planning."

The Last Kings of Thule, by Jean Malaurie. *Parabola*, May 1983, 118, 120.

The Clam Lake Papers, by Edward Lueders. *Western Humanities Review*, Summer 1983, 160–61.

"Life on a Small Scale." Rev. of *In a Patch of Fireweed*, by Bernd Heinrich. *New York Times Book Review*, April 22, 1984, 16.

Indian Country, by Peter Matthiessen. *Outside*, June 1984, 91–92.

Make Prayers to the Raven, by Richard Nelson. *Orion Nature Quarterly*, Summer 1984, 63.

"Recommended Reading." Rev. of *The Peregrine*, by John Baker; *The View from the Oak*, by Judith and Herbert Kohl; *The Falconer of Central Park*, by Donald Knowler; *Make Prayers to the Raven*, by Richard Nelson; and *The Desert*, by John Van Dyke. *Orion Nature Quarterly*, Summer 1987, 59–60.

"Columbus for the Imagination." Rev. of *Follow the Dream*, by Peter Sis; *Christopher Columbus: The Great Adventure and How We Know about It*, by Delno C. West and Jean M. West; *I Sailed with Columbus*, by Mirian Schlein; *If You Were There in 1492*, by Barbara Brenner; *Columbus and the World around Him*, by Milton Meltzer; *In 1492*, by Jean Marzollo; *Voyages of Columbus*, by Ken Hills; *Christopher Columbus and the First Voyages to the New World*, by Stephen C. Dodge; *I Sailed with Columbus*, by Susan Martin; *The Admiral and the Deck Boy*, by Genevieve A. O'Connor; *The High Voyage*, by Olga Litowinsky; *Discovering Christopher Columbus*, by Kathy Pelta; and *The Discovery of the Americas*, by Betsy and Giulio Maestro. *New York Times Book Review*, November 10, 1991, 29, 56.

Lopez's existing focus on the larger meaning of the then-upcoming quincentennial of Columbus' landfall led him to accept the *Times*'s invitation to review these books written for children, nearly all of which he found wanting.

Shem Pete's Alaska: The Territory of the Upper Cook Inlet Dena'ina, by James Kari and James A. Fall. *Orion*. 26 (January–February 2004), 74–75.

Lopez's first review in thirteen years. The book, which represents the lifework of linguist and anthropologist Kari, a longtime friend, supports ideas central to Lopez's thinking about the need to include indigenous thought in modern politics and social planning.

Forewords, Introductions, and Catalog and Calendar Essays

Sierra Club Wildlife Calendar 1980. New York: Charles Scribner's Sons, 1979. Calendar essay.

Nathan Farb and Michael Jackson. *Galápagos*. New York: Rizzoli, 1989. Introduction, "Life and Death in Galápagos."
The New York Times Magazine commissioned Lopez and the photographer Nathan Farb to produce a piece about the Galápagos Islands. When Lopez declined to accept a number of the magazine's editorial changes, he agreed to let Nathan Farb use the essay as an introduction in this book. The piece appeared simultaneously in *North American Review* (1989).

Stephen Trimble. *The Sagebrush Ocean: A Natural History of the Great Basin*. Reno: University of Nevada Press, 1989. Foreword.

Alan Magee. *Alan Magee Inlets*. Portland, ME: Joan Whitney Pason Gallery of Art, 1990. Catalog essay.

Joseph Holmes. *Natural Light: American Photographers Collection*. Berkeley, CA: The Nature Company / Yolla Bolly Press, 1990. Foreword.

Tiana Bighorse. *Bighorse the Warrior*. Tucson: University of Arizona Press, 1990. Foreword.

Richard Nilsen. *Helping Nature Heal*. Berkeley, CA: Ten Speed Press, 1991. Foreword.

Joseph Barbato and Lisa Weinerman, eds. *Heart of the Land: Essays on Last Great Places*. New York: Pantheon, 1995. Foreword.

Mercedes Dorson and Jeanne Wilmot. *Tales from the Rain Forest: Myths and Legends from the Amazonian Indians of Brazil*. Hopewell, NJ: Ecco Press, 1997. Foreword.

Richard Rowland. *Mind of the Dragon*. Astoria, OR: Clatsop Community College, 1997. Exhibition catalog. Foreword.
Lopez wrote the foreword to this catalog for a show devoted to the practices of a group of potters working with an anagama, or wood-fired, kiln in Oregon's Coast Range, a community he wrote about in "Before the Temple of Fire" (1998).

Lillian Pitt. *Spirits Keep Whistling Me Home: The Works of Lillian Pitt*. Warm Springs, OR: Museum of Warm Springs, 1999. Exhibition catalog. Essay, "Listening to Lillian."

Charles Kogod and Barbara Payne, eds. *Heart of a Nation: Writers and Photographers Inspired by the American Landscape.* Washington, D.C.: National Geographic Society, 2000. Introduction, "Looking Homeward."

Ken Lopez. *Nature Writing: A Catalog.* Hadley, MA: K. Lopez, 2000. Introduction, "Nature Writing."
Bookseller Ken Lopez (no relation) asked Barry Lopez to write the introduction to this special issue of his catalog series.

Charles Hobson. *Why I Love Books: The Artworks of Charles Hobson.* Bolinas, CA: Bolinas Museum, 2002. Introduction, "The Compass Rose."

Rebecca Dobkins. *Rick Bartow: My Eye.* Salem, OR: Hallie Ford Museum of Art, Willamette University, 2002. Exhibition catalog. Foreword, "Straight with the Medicine."
"My contribution, an essay, chronicles a day-long visit with Bartow, my longtime friend, advisor, and collaborator."

Guy Maynard and Kathleen Holt, eds. *Best Essays NW: Perspectives from Oregon Quarterly Magazine.* Eugene: University of Oregon Press, 2003. Foreword.

Philip Zaleski, ed. *The Best American Spiritual Writing 2005.* Boston: Houghton Mifflin, 2005. Introduction.

Barry Lopez and Debra Gwartney, eds. *Home Ground: Language for an American Landscape.* San Antonio, TX: Trinity University Press, 2006. Introduction.

Emily Neff. *The Modern West: American Landscapes, 1890–1950.* New Haven, CT: Yale University Press, 2006. Introduction, "Out West."

Barry Lopez. *The Future of Nature: Writing on a Human Ecology from Orion Magazine.* Minneapolis: Milkweed Editions, 2007. Introduction.

2009 Wildlife Australia. Hobart, Tasmania: The Wilderness Society, 2008. Calendar essay, "Emancipation."

John Fowles. *The Tree.* New York: Ecco Press, 2010. Introduction.

Stephen Bogener and William Tydeman, eds. *Llano Estacado: An Island in the Sky.* Lubbock: Texas Tech University Press, 2011. Introduction.

Outside. Santa Rosa, CA: Nawakum Press, 2013. Afterword.

Interviews

Nicholas O'Connell, *Seattle Review,* 1985.
Jim Aton, *Western American Literature,* 1986.
Nicholas O'Connell, *The Field's End,* 1987.
Kay Bonetti, *Missouri Review,* 1988.

Patrick Nunally, *North Dakota Quarterly,* 1988.

Edward Lueders and E. O. Wilson, *Writing Natural History,* 1989.

Ray Gonzalez, *Bloomsbury Review,* 1990.

Ken Margolis, *Orion,* 1990.

Alice Evans, *Poets & Writers,* 1994.

John Murray, *Bloomsbury,* 1998.

Paul Kirman, *Baybury Review,* 1998.

David Thomas Sumner, *Weber Studies,* 2001.

Diane Oben, *The Book That Changed My Life,* 2002.

Daniel J. Philippon, *Ruminator Review,* 2002–2003.

Alan Magee, *Alan Magee,* 2003.

Greg Barrios, *Nature Conservancy,* 2003.

William Tydeman, *Iron Horse Literary Review,* 2003.

Donna Seaman, *Writers on the Air,* 2005.

Michael Shapiro, *Michigan Quarterly Review,* 2005.

William Tydeman, *Northwest Review,* 2006.

Michael Shapiro, *The Sun,* 2006. [Excerpted and edited version of his *Michigan Quarterly Review* interview of 2005.]

Christian Martin, *Georgia Review,* 2006.

Terry Gross, *Fresh Air,* 2013.

Broadsides

"A Short Manifesto." Portfolio, 1984. Collection of broadsides published in an edition of 100–125 by Copper Canyon Press, Port Townsend, Washington. Work by Ishmael Reed, Margaret Atwood, William Stafford, Charles Wright, Tess Gallagher, Mark Strand, Marvin Bell, Carolyn Kizer, Graeme Gibson, Lewis Hyde, Jim Heynen, and Barry Lopez. All were participants in the 1984 Port Townsend Writers Workshop.

"The image I carry of Cortés . . ." Oakland, CA: Okeanos Press, 1990. From "The Passing Wisdom of Birds." Published in an edition of 250. Designed and printed by Eric Johnson in association with Black Oak Books on the occasion of a reading by Lopez on Earth Day 1990.

"The stories people tell . . ." St. Paul, MN: Hungry Mind Bookstore, 1990. Badger's saying about "story" from *Crow and Weasel.* Published in an edition of 100 signed and numbered copies on the occasion of a reading at the University of Minnesota, March 15, 1990.

Untitled. Badger's saying about "story" from *Crow and Weasel,* 1990 or 1991.

Small, untitled broadside. Published in an edition of 80–100 by Okeanos Press, Berkeley, CA, for a private client, David Rich, to be given to guests at a gathering for a reading by someone at his home in Berkeley.

Untitled. 1991. Quote from *Arctic Dreams*. No further information.

Without Regret. 1991. Sentence from a paragraph in "Searching for Ancestors" in *Crossing Open Ground*. Incorporated into a painting by Elizabeth Gallery and printed by her in her studio at Santa Barbara, CA. Artist's proof edition of 23 (marked "AP"). Total edition limited to 1,000.

Untitled. Paragraph from *Arctic Dreams*, p. 228, slightly rewritten, printed on a "landscape paperwork," 16 × 24 inches high. A collaboration with Amanda Degener, Mary Lyn Nutting, and Claire Van Vliet, utilizing Asian fibers and inclusion techniques to create a dawn sky behind mountains with mist rising. West Burke, VT: Janus Press, 1992. Edition of 90 copies, each sheet unique.

Untitled. 1993. Keepsake broadside. Quote from "Informed by Indifference" (1988). No further information.

Untitled. Artists and Writers Portfolio, United States Antarctic Program/ National Science Foundation, 1993. A collection of 21 broadsides by 21 artists and writers, including twelve color reproductions of paintings and photographs and one black-and-white photographic reproduction, together with eight text statements, all on coated stock, 8½ × 11 inches, the portfolio including a folded sheet describing the Artists and Writers in Antarctic program. Edition of 1,000. Excerpts from "Informed by Indifference" (1988).

Occupancy. A Morning Star Portfolio, vol. 3, no. 4. Edinburgh, Scotland: Morning Star Press, December 1993. Printed and distributed August 1994. Published in an edition of 300, including 26 signed and lettered by the author. Essay and map by the author, hand-drawn and annotated. Approximately 100 additional copies marked O/S for "out of series" printed and distributed to friends of the author and the press, primarily. Edited, designed, and published by Alec Finlay. Three photographs by Kate Joost.

Barry Lopez [2002]. Three sentences from *The Rediscovery of North America*. Published on the occasion of his delivery of the second annual Esther Freier Lecture at the University of Minnesota, March 15, 2002. Red Dragonfly Press, Northfield, Minnesota. Designed and printed by Scott King. Edition size unknown.

Untitled. Badger's saying about "story" from *Crow and Weasel*. Published in an edition of 100. Printed on ochre-colored Yatsuo paper from Japan, handset in Gill Sans type. Designed, printed, and published by Sandy Tilcock at lone goose press in Eugene, Oregon, 2004.

Untitled. 2004. Keepsake broadside. Paragraph from "Apocalypse" in *Resistance*. Published in an edition of 100 copies, numbered and signed, by Grey Spider Press, Cedro Wooley, Washington, for Third Place Books, Seattle, Washington, June 8, 2004. On the occasion of a reading by Lopez.

"Once I was asked by a seatmate . . ." Keepsake broadside. Excerpt from "A Voice" in *About This Life*. Published in an edition of 100 by The Press at Colorado College, Colorado Springs, Colorado, to commemorate a reading by Lopez on April 15, 2005.

"Barry Lopez" [2005]. Three paragraphs from "Apocalypse" in *Resistance*. Published in an edition of 100 numbered and signed copies by lone goose press, Eugene, Oregon, September 2005. Handset Gill Sans type and Declaration of Independence graphic printed on Hahnemuhle Bugra paper.

"The Trail." Designed, printed, and assembled by Paul Moxon at Penland School for Crafts, Penland, North Carolina, November 2011. An edition of 35. Text appeared first at www.350.org in 2009 and subsequently in the January/February issue of *Orion*.

"Barry Lopez." Keepsake broadside, designed by Suzie Rouzie, printed by Cathy DeForest at her Jubilation Press, Ashland, Oregon, April 20, 2012. An eighty-three word excerpt from "Introduction" in *River Notes: The Dance of Herons*. Edition of 120, signed by Lopez and numbered. Published to commemorate the author's appearance April 20–23, 2012, sponsored by Chautauqua Poets and Writers of Ashland.

CPSIA information can be obtained at www.ICGtesting.com
Printed in the USA
LVOW07s2330110214

373250LV00002B/2/P